Artisan Cake Company's Visual Guide to
CAKE DECORATING

ELIZABETH MAREK

Race Point Publishing
An imprint of Quarto Publishing Group USA Inc.
276 Fifth Avenue, Suite 206
New York, New York 10001

RACE POINT PUBLISHING and the distinctive Race Point Publishing logo
are trademarks of Quarto Publishing Group USA Inc.

EDITOR Susan Sulich
DESIGNER Tim Palin Creative

PHOTO CREDITS
Krissy Allori Photography: Back cover, pages 13, 31 (right), 32, 37, 39, 96, 108, 112, 126, 136 (top), 146, 180, 192,
and all instructional photography (unless otherwise noted)

Elizabeth Marek: 4–5, 7, 8, 19, 28–30, 31 (left), 34 (top), 35, 41, 46–51, 70, 71 (right), 77 (top, bottom right), 78 (right), 79 (top left, center right), 81 (top right), 84 (center right), 87, 88 (top left), 91 (bottom right), 92–95, 99 (left), 100, 101 (top left, bottom right); 104, 105 (top, bottom right), 110–111, 113, 114–118, 122–125, 134–135, 136 (bottom), 137–141, 142–143, 154–169, 170, 204

Paul Rich Studio: Front cover, 1, 16, 17, 18, 217; **Simi Cakes & Confections**: 12; **Stacy Dugan-Urbina**: 72 (left); **Michelle Curran**: 73 (left); **Bonnie Vaughn**: 74 (left); **Adam Trujillo Photography**: 77 (bottom left), 89; **Donna Rupinski**: 78 (left); **Melissa Olson**: 79 (bottom left); **Michelle Boyd, Good Gracious Cakes**: 79 (bottom right), 90 (right), 107; **Tammy Navarre**: 80 (top left); **Jacki Fanto, Blissfully Sweet**: 80 (bottom right), 84 (bottom right); **Barbara Reed**: 81 (top left); **Laura Ferdinandy Talbot**: 82 (left); **Hazelwood Photo**: 82 (right); **Brenda Bond**: 83 (left); **Mandi Buckalew**: 84 (top left); **Jessica Harris**: 84 (center left), 86 (top right); **Anna Wawzonek, Anna Elizabeth Cakes**: 85 (left); **Sarah Myers, High Five Cakes**: 85 (right); **Ann-Marie Youngblood, Ann-Marie's Cakes**: 86 (top left); **Kasey Smith, Kakes by Klassic**: 86 (bottom right); **Keren Maxwell, iced by Kez**: 88 (bottom left); **Kara Andretta, Kara's Couture Cakes**: 88 (right); **Mayen Orido, Way Beyond Cakes by Mayen**: 90 (left); **Kara Bustos, Sift by Kara**: 91 (top); **Michelle Honeman**: 91 (bottom left); **Avalon Yarnes, Avalon Cakes**: 99 (right); **Alyssa Hall, Cuteology Cakes**: 101 (top right, bottom left); **Ruth Rickey**: 105 (bottom left); **Thinkstock**: Backgrounds throughout.

All cakes made by **Artisan Cake Company**, unless otherwise noted (see page 224). All cake illustrations by **Elizabeth Marek**.

ISBN-13: 978-1-937994-69-3

Printed in China

2 4 6 8 10 9 7 5 3 1

www.racepointpub.com

CONTENTS

INTRODUCTION

My first cake for another person, 2008

My first sculpted cake, 2009

My first attempt at a stacked cake, 2009

I didn't start out as a cake decorator. After high school I spent several years bouncing from job to job, not ever finding that perfect fit. (In my lifetime, I have had over sixty jobs!) I felt adrift. Soon after my twenty-fourth birthday, I enrolled in a graphic design program. Three years later, I graduated near the top of my class and landed a job as Art Director at a marketing and advertising agency. I was completely satisfied for about two years, and then it started again. The job ceased to feel creative, and my days were becoming increasingly stressful and boring.

One day I was relaxing by watching one of my favorite shows, *Ace of Cakes*. The show is about a small bakery that is basically run by a down-to-earth guy gone baker and his group of friends. Every day was filled with amazing cakes that defied gravity and imagination. I had never even known that it was possible to create cakes like this. What was even better, the people in the bakery all seemed so happy, laughing even when something went wrong. They would band together to get the problem fixed. I loved every minute of it. I casually said to my husband one day, "I wish I could just bake and decorate cakes all day like that." His response changed my life. He simply replied, "Why can't you?" I often wonder if he regretted saying that to me because I quit my job and started baking full time after only six months of practicing. And so it began.

When I first started decorating cakes, I somehow got it in my head that there was a "right way" and a "wrong way" to do everything. Every time I ran into a problem or had a "caketastrophe," I would feel so frustrated and think, "If only I knew how the professionals do it!" This was before the days of cake groups and online tutorials. There was little you could find on the web in the way of step-by-step instructions. I became extremely frustrated that I could not find specific information like the perfect cake recipe or what kind of buttercream I should be using. I would read cake blogs and ask questions in the comments, only to be verbally bashed for DARING to ask a pro for his or her secrets! I was at a loss. How was I to ever learn anything? I purchased a lot of books during this time as well but felt that the information was always lacking. They would show how-tos and ideas for decorating cakes, but I always felt key steps were missing. How does that icing get so smooth? Where do you buy those tools from? What happens if something goes wrong? I started practicing making cakes on my own, but they really were horrendous. Sloppy corners, terrible piping, and cracked fondant, but I was having a blast experimenting and I kept on going!

I began making cakes for everyone's events: birthdays, baby showers, bachelorette parties—I was always bringing the cake! I even made a few wedding cakes for friends and family members. Like many other bakers, I just muddled my way through cake after cake, figuring things out by trial and error as best I could. They say with every mistake, you learn a lesson. Some lessons are harder to learn than others.

My first paid wedding cake was not the first wedding cake I had ever made, so I did not feel particularly nervous about the delivery. I was very happy with how the cake turned out and even got to make some lovely sugar flowers for the first time. The cake was super small, only three tiers, so I decided to decorate and stack the entire cake before I delivered it. At this time I knew very little about making cakes from scratch (other than the fact that I was terrible at it), so I was still using box mixes. My bride requested champagne cake, and I said yes first and looked up a recipe later. Supposedly all I had to do was replace a little of the liquids with champagne. It seemed easy enough. I baked up a couple of layers and they looked beautiful. Nice and fluffy and smelled divine.

The day before delivery I torted my cakes, filled them with Bavarian cream (a vanilla custard), and iced them with American buttercream. I used wooden dowels to stack my cake. I figured I didn't need that many since it was so small (plus they were really hard to cut!), so I only used four dowels. After I had the cake decorated and stacked, I inserted all the tulips that I spent hours working on into the cake. I didn't know at the time that it was not good to put wires directly into a cake. Thankfully there was no acidity in the cake so it would not have been a problem, but looking back on that, I cringe! (Always wrap wires in floral tape before inserting into a cake.)

On the day of the wedding, I made SO many mistakes. My dad drove me to the venue, and I held the cake in my hands because I did not think to put the cake in a box and did not want to put it on the floor of the car. The first thing I learned is that your lap is not a stable place to put anything. The venue was not far away but within five minutes of leaving the house, I could see that the middle tier was bulging on one side. I did not want to believe what was happening, so I held my breath and hoped it would be okay.

It was not okay. By the time we reached the venue, the middle tier was completely collapsing! I tried to stay

My first paid wedding cake with its beautiful sugar flowers sadly never made it to the wedding.

calm and asked at the site if there was a kitchen I could use for a moment to touch up the cake. I quickly realized the problem. My cake was so light, it could not support the weight of my sugar flowers. I had so many flowers that the wires literally vibrated their way through the cake and cut it into a million pieces internally. The four dowels I had placed inside did not do much to stop the cake from collapsing.

There was no way to save the cake. My hands were shaking as I began to pull the sugar tulips out of my crumbling cake. I was panicked. I had no idea what to do. I wasn't a big bakery. I couldn't run back home and pick up more cake. There wasn't time! I called the only number I had memorized (this was before cell phones were so popular) and asked my sister to go to the nearest bakery and beg for a premade cake round that I could use to replace the broken layer.

Amazingly she was able to get one, along with some buttercream. I recoated the cake in buttercream and covered the entire tier in the sugar tulips to cover the buttercream. Let me just say, it looked HORRIBLE. I let the bride's mother know the problem and told her I was doing everything I could to get her daughter a replacement cake. She did not seem too upset, thankfully, just concerned.

After an hour of frantic redecorating, I brought the cake out into a packed reception with all eyes on me. My face was burning. I heard the father of the bride say casually to the mother of the bride as I walked by, "I thought the cake was supposed to be here two hours ago?" The mother of the bride gave him a look, and I could not bear to meet their eyes. I left more embarrassed than I have ever been in my life. I went home and just cried. I thought I would never get past that moment. It still makes my stomach hurt thinking about it now, six years later.

I learned numerous lessons doing that one delivery. I learned the importance of properly supporting your tiers before transporting, to apply sugar flowers after delivery, and to stack on-site. I learned that chilling my cakes before delivery helps to keep things stable, and that box mix cake, while tasty, is not the best for wedding cakes because it is so light and fluffy. I also learned the importance of having an emergency kit for cake deliveries, which, if I had it that day, would have saved me a lot of heartache. Most of all, I realized that there are no shortcuts to a perfect cake and there are no "perfect ways" of doing anything.

I also learned that people can be really, really amazing. After the event, I contacted the father of the bride who had paid for the wedding cake and offered him a complete refund and a heartfelt apology. He would not accept my money. In fact, he told me he was proud of me for being brave enough to stay as long as I did to try and fix the cake and provide his daughter with something the day of her wedding rather than admitting defeat and leaving the burden of finding a replacement cake on them. He told me to keep up my hard work and not to let this setback stop me from pursuing my career as a cake decorator. I will never, ever forget that phone call.

So I took my lumps and moved on. I made changes to the way I approached every facet of making cakes from that moment on. I decided to go back to school to get my baking and pastry arts degree at Oregon Culinary Institute. The information I gained there was so valuable and completely changed the quality of the cakes I was creating for my clients. I suddenly knew why a recipe did not work out and was able to take a recipe and tweak it successfully to my own liking. I even created a fondant recipe made from marshmallows that I still use to this day. It is often a key piece in convincing clients to order my cakes over a competitor because my fondant actually tastes good. I reached out to other cake decorators and made friendly connections so I could learn more about how they approached cake decorating and what worked and didn't work for them.

Soon my business was flourishing. The first two years were a blur. I had no idea what I was doing. I overbooked myself constantly. I never said no to an order. I was constantly trying to learn new techniques. I was more tired than I had ever been in my life, but I was also so extremely happy. My clients were thrilled with their cakes, and I was getting more business than I could handle.

During my third year in business, I was working so many long hours that I was getting really burnt out. I decided to take a small break from baking and decorating and once again focus on learning. I had recently discovered some online cake groups where people freely discussed techniques. What a gold mine! I tried not to be that annoying person who was always asking questions. Occasionally I would answer questions myself and was surprised that I knew more than I thought—trial and error had paid off. I started casually teaching some private classes locally as well as making some simple online tutorials. People would ask questions in the comment section, and I would answer each and every single one. I started doing the same on my social media page and got a lot of great interaction with newbie cake decorators asking for advice. I would always answer and was surprised to hear that I was one of the few who would share their knowledge. Something clicked inside me. I discovered that, in addition to making cakes, I loved to learn, and I love to share that knowledge with others.

My cakes are my medium. I naturally lean towards sculpted cakes and edible toppers.

above: *Because of my graphic design training and drawing experience, I am able to mock up professional-looking cake sketches for my clients that show exact style, color, and details.*

right: *Finished cake created for the bride: hand-painted tiers, fondant ruffles, and sugar flowers.*

My cakes are my medium. I naturally lean towards sculpted cakes and edible toppers. I am always experimenting with new ways to create a sturdy cake structure or experimenting with edible ingredients to create the textures and colors that I want. My years as a graphic artist greatly enhanced my ability to design visually impressive cakes. I am inspired by things around me—feathers, flowers, watercolor, jewelry—and love to re-create what I see in cake form. Nothing is off-limits.

After six years of cake decorating, I have never felt more passionate about what I do. I learn something new every single day. Maybe that is what keeps it exciting for me. It never gets boring. I have the pleasure of traveling to teach classes all over as well as interacting with other amazing cake artists. I have a backlog of dozens of tutorials ready to go up online. I am addicted to social media because it allows me to connect with so many other decorators. I still remember how frustrating it was for me to learn the small steps that took me from beginner to professional. I have dedicated this book to those memories. I have carefully selected projects that will help you refine your skills and take them to the next level. The projects range from easy to advanced, so you can work your way up or start at the level where you feel most comfortable.

You will also notice little notes throughout this book that are called "Pro Tips." They are actual tips from cake decorating industry professionals who are tops in their field. These are the little tidbits that always gave me that "ah-ha!" moment when I was learning. These tips may help you troubleshoot common problems or simply make a technique easier.

I hope you enjoy this book and, as always, I am available on social media through any of the links below if you have any questions. I am honored to help budding artists and cake decorators reach their creative goals and look forward to seeing the amazing projects you all create.

—Elizabeth Marek

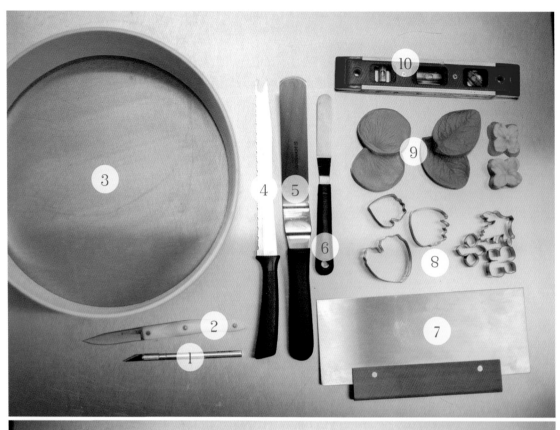

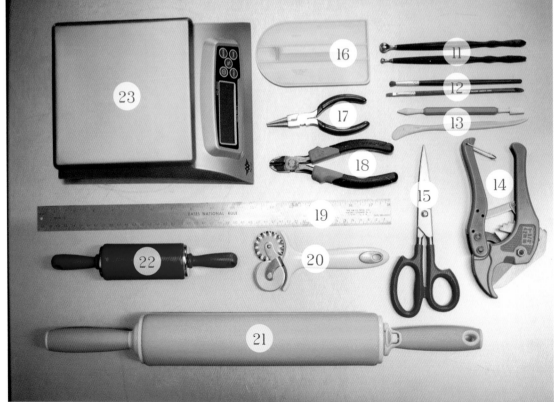

TOOLS OF THE TRADE

MUST-HAVE EQUIPMENT

These are tools I use almost every day for every cake project. Some of them are very simple and others have specialized uses, but I could not live without any of them.

1. X-ACTO knife
2. Sharp utility knife
3. Large powdered-sugar sifter
4. Sharp serrated knife
5. Offset spatula
6. Mini offset spatula
7. Tall bench scraper
8. High-quality metal cutters
9. High-quality veiners and molds
10. Level
11. Metal ball tools in various sizes
12. Petal dust brushes
13. Sculpting tools
14. PVC cutters
15. Heavy-duty
    kitchen scissors
16. Plastic fondant smoothers
17. Rounded jewelry pliers/
    needle-nose pliers
18. Wire cutters
19. Metal ruler
20. Pastry wheel
21. Large rolling pin
22. Small rolling pin
23. Scale
24. Turntable (right)

BAKER'S SECRET

To make my cakes and frostings, I use a scale and weigh all my ingredients, including liquids. I find using volume for measurement incredibly inaccurate. Many factors, such as how you sift your dry ingredients or the humidity on the day you're baking, can greatly affect the amount of an ingredient you end up with if you're measuring by volume. Baking is a science, and small changes in ingredients can affect the outcome of your recipe in a big way. Invest in a scale, and you'll find that your cakes will turn out consistently good every time.

NICE TO HAVE

Every decorator has his or her basic go-to tools, but beyond those are the super tools. I don't have a lot of fancy tools and products in my kitchen, but the few I have are worth it because they can cut hours of work off a project and/or reduce the pain in your back and neck. They can mean the difference between an amateurish- or flawless-looking cake and the difference between five hours of work or five minutes.

Ready-to-Use Isomalt

Isomalt can be intimidating for the beginner. I struggled for years with cloudiness, stickiness, and crystallization until I started using premade isomalt. I adore the super-clear, premade isomalt from Simi Cakes. It melts so easily with no bubbles or cloudiness. It cools quickly and is easy to work with.
wwww.simicakes.com

Airbrush

Once you start using an airbrush, you will wonder how you ever got by without one. My favorite is the airbrush by Steven Barela. It allows for awesome detail and good control over the spray, which is so important. He is also an amazing cake artist himself and uses his own product.
www.barelagrafix.com

Digital Camera

Before my cakes go out the door to fulfill their cake destiny, I always take a photo. Even if you bake purely for pleasure, it's good to have a record of the cakes you've made to show family and friends if they want you to make something specific.

premade isomalt

Photography Backdrop

I love the quality and the price of Lemondrop Stop's beautiful backdrops. They are made of lightweight synthetic material that feels like paper but is durable enough to use over and over. Just tape to a wall and roll up when done.
www.lemondropstop.com

Electric Pasta Machine

Pasta machines make working with gumpaste and fondant so much easier and give much more consistent results. The Roma Electric Pasta Machine from Weston is less expensive than mixer attachments, and it frees up both hands to easily guide gumpaste or fondant through. Plus it allows you to roll it super thin.
www.westonsupply.com

Sugar Dress

Sugar Dress is a product that lets you create lace and intricate looks on your cakes without hours and hours of piping. The product stays flexible for weeks and can be used in large pieces or trimmed down for use as accents.
www.sugardelites.com

Mini Silicone Mat

This mat has multiple uses in a baker's kitchen. You can use it to roll out gumpaste, keep a cake from sliding while you ice it, or even pour isomalt on it. It's all I use for rolling out gumpaste or making figures. The larger mats work too, but they are cumbersome.
www.ruthrickeyproducts.gostorego.com

Marvelous Molds

These food-safe, silicone molds create intricate patterns, textures, and borders out of fondant seamlessly and effortlessly. They also make gorgeous isomalt brooches, tiaras, and beads. There are many molds to choose from, and tutorials to show you how to use them. Best of all, they are extremely affordable and high quality.
www.marvelousmolds.com

Sugar Dress

silicone mold

DIY EQUIPMENT

Over the years there were times when I would find I needed something to accomplish a specific task that would make my job easier, only to discover no such item existed on the commercial market. So I found a way to make those special tools myself. These are a few of the ones I use most frequently. They are made from readily available and often repurposed materials. A small investment of time and effort will give you a tool that will pay back in many hours saved and a much better-looking finished cake.

Flower Holder

When making flower centers or applying the first layer of petals, you need to have a place to put them to dry. Purchase a round of floral foam (white, not green). It has a hard, crunchy texture. Poke a few fat straws into the foam and voilà, a place to hold flower stems until they dry.

Petal Dryer

Flower petals are cup shaped. It's a challenge to get them to dry and keep their shape. Glue plastic spoons onto a cake board and place your wired petals into them to dry. I have three or four of these and use them for everything from petals to leaves to curved toppers.

Egg Foam

You can find this foam in the bedding aisle, or sometimes it comes with electronics as a packing material. It's the perfect shape for forming natural leaves or letting small things dry without fear of sticking.

Hanging Flower Rack

I use cupboard shelf dividers as flower racks when drying flowers upside down. You can also use cookie cooling racks if they have legs or can be positioned between two supports.

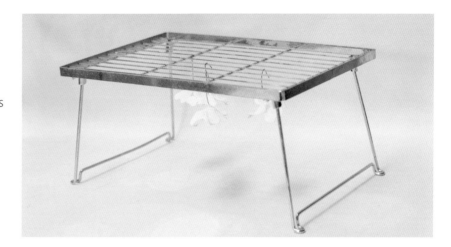

Airbrush Booth

One of the first "OOPS!" moments I ever had was the day I decided to airbrush a cake blue in my kitchen. I didn't realize it at the time, but I was literally blowing blue food color into every crevice in my entire kitchen. I couldn't tell right away, but as soon as the counter got wet, or I touched a pan, a smear of bright blue would appear. I desperately needed an airbrush booth but could not afford a professional-grade one. I decided to take matters into my own hands and made my own booth. It did take some doing, but overall I am very happy with it and still use it to this day. For complete directions on how to make the airbrush booth go to www.artisancakecompany.com/2014/05/airbrush-booth-tutorial

CHAPTER 1

CAKE AND FROSTING RECIPES

One of the first things that I learned in pastry school was not the perfect cake recipe. It was how to read and execute a recipe. We refer to this as the "method." When trying out a new recipe, you must read the method first all the way through to familiarize yourself with the process. Every step is important, and you cannot skip any steps. Most of the questions I receive posted online about my recipes are related to "I forgot to do step A, will it still work?" The short answer is "No." Your cake might turn out okay, but in reality, it usually won't—and it definitely won't be as good as it would have been if you had followed all the steps. So save yourself some heartache, and always read the recipe completely before you begin.

The second most important step is to gather your ingredients. We call this *mise en place*, which is French for "everything in its place." There is nothing worse than getting halfway through your recipe and realizing you don't have any more baking powder left. Gather your ingredients ahead of time, and set them out in front of you. This will help you visualize each step while you are going through the recipe. You are less likely to miss a step if you don't have to stop and hunt for an ingredient.

CAKE RECIPES

The following recipes have been my go-to ones for years. They are great for stacking, carving, or just eating warm out of the oven (not that I ever do that!). The key ingredient in these cakes is the butter. Butter helps keep cakes moist and also acts as a stabilizer for carving. Note: These cakes do not taste their best cold. So make sure you allow time for refrigerated cakes to come to room temperature before eating, or they will seem dry. Also be careful not to overbake. Contrary to popular baking wisdom, if the cakes are shrinking from the sides of the pan, they are overbaked. The cakes are done when a toothpick inserted in the center comes out with just a couple of sticky crumbs on it.

Baker's Secret

Any of the following cake recipes can be converted to cupcakes. Omit the oil or they will be too moist and the wrappers will pull away. Fill your wrappers 3/4 of the way full and bake at 330°F/166°C for about 20 minutes. Check after 15 minutes. Oil-proof wrappers work best if you are having problems with your cupcake wrappers pulling away from your cake.

TENDER VANILLA CAKE

This recipe is the base for most of my cake recipes. You can see the variations on page 22. Tweaking the spices or even adding a small amount of a dry ingredient, like nuts or berries, can dramatically change a cake. Every baked-good recipe is a delicate balance of dry/wet/sugar/fat ratios. Substitutions or additions have to be done carefully and in relation to the other components in the recipe. If you alter one type of ingredient too much, the recipe will not work anymore. For example, you may think that you can just replace water with an equal amount of soda, but the recipe won't turn out right because of the added sugar content from the soda. If you take out the butter and add applesauce, the consistency may not be the same because of the change in fat content. Try to replace fats with fats, sugars with sugars, etc., in addition to keeping the wet and dry amounts the same, and your recipes should turn out okay.

Yield: Two 8-in/20-cm round cakes

Ingredients:

8 oz/227 g whole milk

3 large eggs

2 oz/57 g vegetable oil

2 tsp vanilla extract

9 oz/255 g granulated sugar

9 oz/255 g cake flour

1 tbsp + 1 tsp baking powder

¾ tsp salt

6 oz/170 g unsalted butter
    (room temperature)

1. Heat oven to 335°F/168°C–350°F/177°C. I tend to use the lower setting to prevent my cakes from getting too dark on the outside before the inside is done baking. Your temperature may be different, depending on your oven. Start with 350°F/177°C and work your way down as you experiment. Your cakes should be golden brown but not hard and dark.

2. Measure out liquid ingredients and place them into a bowl and set aside.

3. Measure out dry ingredients and place them into the bowl of the mixer.

4. Attach the paddle to the mixer, and turn on slowest speed. Slowly add chunks of your softened butter until it is all added. Let mix until batter resembles coarse sand.

5. Add ⅓ of your liquid ingredients while mixing on low until just moistened. This part is crucial. Don't add too much liquid.

6. Increase mixing speed to medium. Let the mixture whip up until it has thickened and lightened in color. It should look like soft-serve ice cream. If you do not let the batter mix fully, you will end up with very short, crumbly cakes. This mixing can take up to two minutes. It is important not to undermix or overmix your batter.

7. Scrape the bowl. This is an important step. If you skip it, you will have hard lumps of flour and unmixed ingredients in your batter. If you do it later, they will not mix in fully.

8. Slowly add in the rest of your liquid ingredients, stopping to scrape the bowl one more time halfway through. Your final batter should be thick and not too runny. I have to spoon mine into pans with a rubber spatula.

1. Stir cocoa powder and boiling water until cocoa is dissolved. Allow to cool completely.

2. Heat oven to 335°F/168°C–350°F/177°C. I tend to use the lower setting to prevent my cakes from getting too dark on the outside before the inside is done baking. Your temperature may be different, depending on your oven. Start with 350°F/177°C and work your way down as you experiment. Your cakes should be golden brown but not hard and dark.

3. Measure out liquid ingredients and place them into a bowl, including cocoa mixture, and set aside.

4. Measure out dry ingredients and place them into the bowl of the mixer.

5. Attach your paddle to your mixer, and turn on slowest speed. Slowly add chunks of your softened butter until it is all added. Let mix until batter resembles coarse sand.

6. Slowly add about ⅓ of your liquids while mixing on low until *just* moistened. Increase speed to medium. This part is crucial. Let the mixture whip up until it has thickened and lightened in color. It should look like soft-serve ice cream. If you do not let the batter mix fully, you will end up with very short, crumbly cakes. This mixing can take up to two minutes. It is important not to undermix or overmix your batter.

7. Scrape the bowl. This is an important step. If you skip it, you will have hard lumps of flour and unmixed ingredients in your batter. If you do it later, they will not mix in fully.

8. Slowly add in the rest of your liquid ingredients, stopping to scrape the bowl one more time halfway through. Your final batter should be thick and not too runny. I have to spoon mine into pans with a rubber spatula.

9. Lightly grease two 8-in/20-cm round cake pans with vegetable shortening and dust with cake flour. Tap out excess flour. Fill pans ¾ full. Chocolate cakes rise slightly less than the vanilla cakes. I always start by baking for 20 minutes for 8 in/20 cm and smaller cakes and 30 minutes for 9 in/23 cm and larger cakes and then checking for doneness. If the cakes are still really jiggly, I add another 10 minutes. I will check every five after that until I'm close, and then it's every two minutes. Cakes are done when a toothpick inserted in the center comes out with just a few crumbs.

10. Remove cakes from oven. If they are domed up, place a clean tea towel on top, and using an oven mitt, lightly press down until flat. This does not harm the cakes at all and cuts down on waste.

11. After cakes have cooled for 10 minutes or the pans are cool enough to touch, flip the cakes over and remove from the pans onto the cooling racks to cool completely. Wrap in plastic wrap and chill in the refrigerator for about an hour.

12. Once the cakes are chilled, tort, fill, and crumb coat all at once (see Chapter 2). If you do not plan on crumb coating the same day, you can leave the wrapped cakes on the countertop. Chilling can dry out your cakes before they are iced, so avoid keeping them in the refrigerator longer than necessary. Cakes can be frozen in freezer bags for later use as well.

Baker's Secret

Keep in mind that the better the quality of the cocoa powder you use, the better the flavor your cakes and frostings will have.

RED VELVET CAKE

This traditional cake has a fabulously southern flair. The deep red color is no trick, just plain and simple red food coloring and a dash of cocoa powder. The real flavor comes from buttermilk and a little vinegar. It's a moist and tender cake that pairs well with buttercream or classic cream cheese frosting.

Yield: Two 8-in/20-cm round cakes

Ingredients:

3 large eggs

8 oz/227 g buttermilk

2 tbsp red gel food color

1 tbsp vanilla extract

2 oz/57 g vegetable oil

1¼ tsp white vinegar

7 oz/198 g granulated sugar

10 oz/285 g cake flour

1 tbsp cocoa powder

1¼ tsp baking soda

½ tsp salt

2 oz/57 g unsalted butter
(room temp)

1. Heat oven to 335°F/168°C–350°F/177°C. I tend to use the lower setting to prevent my cakes from getting too dark on the outside before the inside is done baking. Your temperature may be different, depending on your oven. Start with 350°F/177°C and work your way down as you experiment. Your cakes should be golden brown but not hard and dark.

2. Measure out liquid ingredients and place them into a bowl and set aside.

3. Measure out dry ingredients and place them into the bowl of the mixer.

4. Attach the paddle to your mixer, and turn on slowest speed. Slowly add chunks of your softened butter until it is all added. Let mix until batter resembles coarse sand.

5. Slowly add about ⅓ of your liquids while mixing on low until *just* moistened. Increase speed to medium. This part is crucial. Let the mixture whip up until it has thickened and lightened in color. It should look like soft-serve ice cream. If you do not let the batter mix fully, you will end up with very short, crumbly cakes. This mixing can take up to two minutes. It is important not to undermix or overmix your batter.

6. Scrape the bowl. This is an important step. If you skip it, you will have hard lumps of flour and unmixed ingredients in your batter. If you do it later, they will not mix in fully.

7. Slowly add in the rest of your liquid ingredients, stopping to scrape the bowl one more time halfway through. Your final batter should be thick and not too runny. I have to spoon mine into pans with a rubber spatula.

8. Lightly grease two 8-in/20-cm round cake pans with vegetable shortening and dust with cake flour. Tap out excess flour. Fill pans ½ full. I always start by baking for 30 minutes and then checking. If the cakes are still really jiggly, I add another 10 minutes. I will check every five after that until I'm close, and then it's every two minutes. Cakes are done when a toothpick inserted in the center comes out with just a few crumbs.

9. Remove cakes from oven. If they are domed up, place a clean tea towel on top, and using an oven mitt, lightly press down until flat. This does not harm the cakes at all and cuts down on waste.

10. After cakes have cooled for 10 minutes or the pans are cool enough to touch, flip the cakes over and remove from the pans onto the cooling racks to cool completely. Wrap in plastic wrap and chill in the refrigerator for about an hour.

11. Once the cakes are chilled in the refrigerator, tort, fill, and crumb coat all at once (see Chapter 2). If you do not plan on crumb coating the same day, you can leave the wrapped cakes on the countertop. Chilling can dry out your cakes before they are iced, so avoid keeping them in the refrigerator longer than necessary. Cakes can be frozen in freezer bags for later use as well.

FROSTINGS AND FILLINGS

A cake without frosting and fillings is really just sweet bread. The following recipes are used in my most popular combinations and are also my personal favorites.

Pro Tip

Edna De la Cruz

www.designmeacake.com

Decorating cakes in warmer climates can be tricky. I live in Florida where we have to deal with heat and humidity. To combat this issue, I use high-ratio shortening in my buttercream to add stability and still keep that silky smooth flavor and texture. The meringue powder also adds stability to the recipe.

If you need a stronger buttercream, one less prone to melting, you can cut the butter in half (or eliminate it completely) and replace it with an equal amount of the high-ratio shortening and a bit of butter extract (start with 1 teaspoon and adjust up to taste).

Replacing all of the butter with the high-ratio shortening and butter extract will result in a pure white buttercream.

CRUSTING BUTTERCREAM

A crusting buttercream is made with powdered sugar and forms a "crust" on the outside so the frosting is not wet to the touch. You can smooth this frosting after it has crusted with a paper towel pressed gently against the buttercream. This recipe by Edna De la Cruz is sweeter than Swiss Meringue Buttercream (see recipe, page 34). Airbrush color adheres to this frosting very well. It contains high-ratio shortening (available from baking or restaurant supply stores), which helps stabilize this frosting in high-temperature areas.

Baker's Secret

You can use coffee creamers in flavors like hazelnut, mocha, caramel, etc. or extracts to flavor your buttercream. Start with 1 teaspoon and increase to taste.

Ingredients:

3.5 oz/99 g high-ratio shortening

4 oz/113 g unsalted butter (room temperature)

1 tsp clear vanilla extract

2 tbsp milk

1 tbsp meringue powder

1 1b/454 g confectioners' sugar

¼ tsp salt

1. In large bowl, cream shortening and butter with electric mixer. For stand mixers, use the paddle attachment, not the whisk.

2. Add vanilla extract and milk.

3. Sift the meringue powder with the sugar into a bowl. Gradually add sugar to mixing bowl, one cup at a time, beating on a slow speed.

4. Scrape sides of bowl often. Add salt and beat on medium until fluffy and light in color. Don't overwhip by beating at a higher speed or you will end up with air bubbles in the icing that will make it impossible to smooth out.

5. Keep bowl covered with a damp cloth until ready to use.

Refrigerated in an airtight container, this icing can be stored for two weeks.

SWISS MERINGUE BUTTERCREAM

Swiss Meringue Buttercream (SMBC) is smooth, rich, light, creamy, and dreamy. It is the buttercream that I use the most. It has a not-too-sweet flavor and a melt-in-your mouth texture. The butter content makes it ideal for chilling and for using on sculpted cakes.

Ingredients:

8 egg whites

1 lb/454 g granulated sugar

½ tsp salt

1 lb/454 g unsalted butter

3.5 oz/99 g solid vegetable shortening

1 tsp vanilla extract

1. Place egg whites and sugar in a mixing bowl over a pot of boiling water.

2. Whisk occasionally. When mixture reaches a temperature of 120°F/49°C (use a thermometer), the sugar is dissolved.

3. Place egg white mixture into the bowl of a stand mixer with a whisk attachment and turn onto high.

4. Add salt and beat until stiff peaks form.

5. Let buttercream cool to room temperature. I will usually take out half of the meringue and place into a cake pan and put both in the refrigerator to cool down faster.

6. Once cooled, add chunks of butter to meringue on medium high and then add the shortening.

7. Let whip until light and fluffy. Add in vanilla extract.

VARIATIONS

Chocolate Buttercream

Add 1 oz/27 g cocoa powder to the buttercream and a splash of dark rum to enhance the chocolate flavor. Whip until combined.

Mint Chocolate Chip

The easy way to do this is to add a touch of mint extract and some mini chocolate chips, but I find that nothing beats fresh mint leaves. I actually infuse my eggs and sugar with two to three sprigs of mint leaves while the sugar is dissolving and then pull out the leaves before whipping. Once the buttercream is whipped up, I add a dab of green food coloring (optional) and a handful of mini chocolate chips—delicious between chocolate cake layers.

Mocha

Brew some extra strong coffee or espresso and chill it. Use a tablespoon or so to flavor buttercream to taste. You can also use instant espresso powder mixed with a little water to get the same results. Add small amounts until you get the taste you like. You can always add more but you can't take it out.

Salted Caramel

This tasty buttercream works great in many flavor combinations. My favorite is ganache, salted caramel buttercream, and vanilla cake. It's like eating a candy bar. Follow the directions for the salted caramel sauce (recipe on page 36). Add two tablespoons to your buttercream (more or less, to suit your tastes).

Lemon Buttercream

You can add lemon curd and some zest to your buttercream but I actually prefer the lemon extract or lemon oil and some zest for this one. I don't like my buttercream too lemony, and the oil really gives it a light flavor.

Strawberry Buttercream

This buttercream is made by adding a couple of tablespoons of strawberry purée (recipe on page 23) to the batch and then whipping it all up until it's nice and fluffy. If your buttercream is breaking, meaning it looks grainy—as if the fats and liquids are separating—heat the bottom of the mixing bowl just a tad with a crème brûlée torch to help combine the two together. It helps to have the buttercream and the purée at the same temperature for even mixing.

SALTED CARAMEL SAUCE

One of my favorite flavors is caramel. I use this sauce on everything: frosting, cupcakes, truffles, ice cream. I might have a slight addiction. After tasting this sauce, you might have one too.

Ingredients:

14 oz/397 g sugar

4 oz/113 g water

6 oz/170 g unsalted butter

8 oz/227 g heavy cream

1 tsp vanilla extract

1 tsp sea salt

1. Combine sugar and water in a saucepan over medium heat.

2. Let come to a boil, whisking occasionally. Cover for five minutes to make sure that all the sugar on the sides of the pan melts and dissolves. Remove the lid. At this point the water is evaporating, and it may take a while to do so completely. Once it has, the bubbles will die down and the sugar will begin to darken in color. Do not walk away—it burns easily.

3. Once the sugar is a nice golden brown, add the butter. It will bubble up, so be careful not to scorch yourself. Whisk until combined.

4. Then add the cream and whisk again.

5. Stir in vanilla extract and salt and let cool before placing in a container to store in the refrigerator. Sauce will thicken as it cools. To thin the sauce, warm it slightly before using.

MARSHMALLOW FONDANT

This Liz Marek Fondant (LMF) is my own recipe that I invented very early on in my career. I was tired of using cheap fondant and tossed around the idea of making my own. I was not happy with the first marshmallow fondant I created because it was not stretchy at all and cracked a lot, but I didn't want to waste it, so I added it to some leftover commercial fondant that I had on hand. The resulting concoction was a beautifully stretchy fondant that worked great. I began tweaking this accidental recipe, and now it is all I use. It rolls super thin, does not tear or get elephant skin, and actually has a good vanilla taste.

Ingredients:

2 lb/907 g confectioners' sugar, sifted

3.5 oz/99 g vegetable shortening

1 lb/454 g mini marshmallows (store-brand marshmallows work best)

2 tbsp warm water (reduce by ½ tbsp for humid areas) or dark food coloring (see Baker's Secret, page 38)

1¼ lb/567 g commercial fondant

1 tsp vanilla extract or other liquid flavorings (optional)

1. Weigh out powdered sugar and sift. If you do not sift, you will have lumps in your fondant that will cause tearing.

2. Place shortening into the bowl of a stand mixer fitted with a dough hook.

3. Begin heating your marshmallows in a large microwave-safe bowl (allow for expansion during heating). Heat for 1 minute on high and stir with a spoon. Heat again for 30 seconds and stir. Heat for 40 seconds more and do not stir.

4. Add water, food coloring, and vanilla or other flavorings if you are using them.

5. Use a spatula to guide the water between the marshmallows and away from the outer edge of the bowl, and then pour into your mixing bowl.

6. Begin mixing on low speed. Add in ½ to ¾ of the confectioners' sugar until a thick paste forms. Let mix until smooth. Add color at this point.

7. Add in one more cup of powdered sugar to get the paste pulling away from the bowl.

8. Heat the commercial fondant for 30 to 40 seconds in microwave on high, until soft.

9. Put a little shortening on your hands. Pull the dough off the hook and scrape out of the mixing bowl into the bowl with the remaining confectioners' sugar.

10. Add in commercial fondant and knead on a table until you can stretch the fondant between your hands like taffy and it does not tear or break. That is how you know it is ready. You may have sugar left over. That's okay. You can use the fondant right away or store it in a plastic bag for months. Heat in the microwave and knead until stretchy before each use.

Baker's Secret

To color fondant lighter colors, make white fondant and add food coloring as desired. For darker colors, omit one tablespoon of water and replace with gel food color (black, red, purple, etc.). If you try to add dark food coloring to fondant after you make it, the color breaks down the fondant and you get pockmarks and tearing.

GANACHE

Ganache is a mixture of chocolate, heavy cream, and a bit of butter. This versatile confection can be melted and poured over cakes or left to firm up to a buttercream-like consistency and used as an icing or filling. When used as an outer coating of frosting on a cake and left to cool in the fridge, it is a great replacement for traditional icing on sculpted cakes because it adds strength to structural elements. A little goes a long way, and it tastes divine with fresh fruits. The ratio I use for ganache is two parts chocolate chips to one part cream. I always use high-quality chocolate for my ganache.

Ingredients:

16 oz/454 g bittersweet or
    milk chocolate

2 tbsp unsalted butter

8 oz/227 g heavy cream

Dash of salt

Splash of rum
    (optional)

1. Measure out chocolate and butter. Set aside in a large bowl.

2. Heat cream, whisking constantly to prevent scorching. As soon as it begins to bubble, remove from the heat and pour over chocolate and butter.

3. Whisk ganache starting from the center in small circles until it all comes together and is smooth and creamy. Stir in salt and rum. Ganache will be soft and liquidy at first. This is the stage when it is great for pouring over iced cakes as a shiny glaze or for dipping cupcakes. Allow the ganache to firm up naturally overnight. Before using, mix with a rubber spatula or in a mixer with a paddle attachment on low speed until creamy. At this stage it will be ready for frosting cakes or piping onto cupcakes.

MODELING CHOCOLATE

Modeling chocolate has many uses. It is great for making figures, building structures, decorating cakes, and making toppers. While it may seem finicky to work with at first, once you get the hang of it, you will find yourself using it in many of your cake designs.

Ingredients:

8 oz/227 g chocolate melts

8 oz/227 g chocolate chips (white, milk, or dark chocolate)

6 oz/170 g corn syrup or glucose

Gel food coloring, if desired

Pro Tip

Mari Senega
www.mssugarart.webs.com

For dark and milk chocolate, I have found that adding 2 tablespoons of low-flavor vegetable oil (safflower, canola oil) to each pound of chocolate used in the recipe helps keep the dark or milk chocolate clay more pliable and not so hard once it sets.

1. Place chocolate melts and chips in heatproof container and melt in microwave. Begin with 30 seconds on high and give it a stir. Continue heating for 15-second intervals. The idea is to heat the chocolate low and slow. You never want it to get too hot.

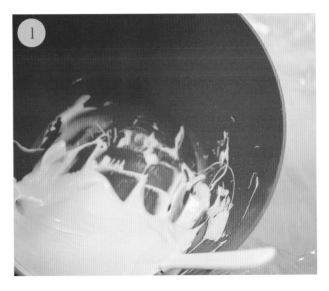

2. Warm the syrup slightly by heating in the microwave for 5 to 10 seconds on high.

3. Add food coloring to the syrup at this point if you are using it.

4. Combine your chocolate and syrup in deep, slow strokes (about 25) with a spatula. Going too fast or mixing too much will begin breaking down your chocolate, and it will get oily. If this happens, you can still save it. Leave your chocolate alone for a few hours or until the oil begins to set and is the consistency of soft butter. Knead the entire batch together and let set until firm.

5. Once the chocolate and syrup are combined, pour onto a piece of plastic wrap. Fold the plastic over to keep the air away from the chocolate.

6. Let the chocolate set partially to the point where it is mostly firm (about 1–3 hours, depending on room temperature) but still bendable and feels like taffy. Knead until smooth and then let set until firm. At this point your modeling chocolate is done.

7. Store chocolate in airtight bags or containers. Modeling chocolate keeps for weeks or months if stored properly. You may need to warm it slightly (no more than 5 seconds) and knead before each use, depending on the temperature of the room.

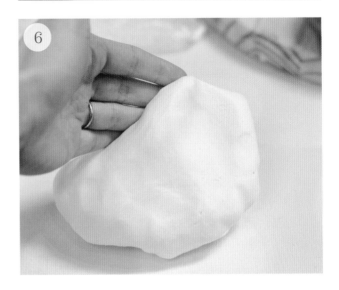

GUMPASTE

Before I really knew much about anything cake related, I knew I wanted to try to make sugar flowers. I purchased a batch of premade gumpaste from my local craft store and proceeded to utterly fail. My gumpaste cracked, it was sticky, and it never really hardened up. I gave up until I found this recipe by Nicolas Lodge. I was amazed at how easy it was to work with and have been using it for all my sugar flowers ever since. It has the perfect ratio of stretchy to softness, and it colors like a dream.

Ingredients:

4 large egg whites

1½–2 lbs/680-907 g confectioners' sugar

1 oz/32 g tylose powder

2–4 tsp solid vegetable shortening, for your hands

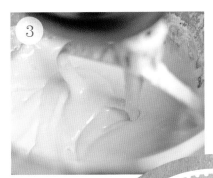
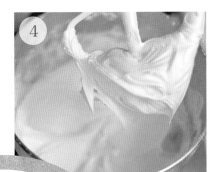

1. Measure out your egg whites and place into the bowl of a stand mixer fitted with a paddle attachment.

2. Break the egg whites up for a few seconds.

3. Turn the mixer onto its lowest setting and begin adding the sugar. Leave out about 1 cup/130 g for later.

4. Turn mixer up to medium speed and let mix until a soft consistency royal icing forms. There should be meringue-like peaks that fall over, and they will be shiny in appearance.

Baker's Secret

Tylose powder and gum tragacanth (or its synthetic version, CMC) are not the same thing. They have different strengths, and if you use the wrong kind, you could end up with a very stiff and crumbly mixture. Make sure you are using a fine-powdered, high-quality tylose powder for your recipe to get the best results.

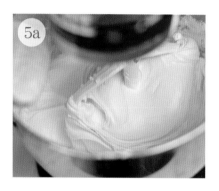

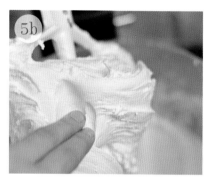

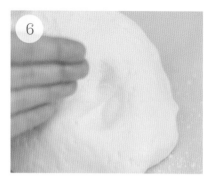

5. Turn the mixer back down to low and slowly begin sprinkling your tylose over the icing (for 5 seconds or so). Turn the speed up to high for a few seconds until the mixture thickens. You should be able to feel the difference when you touch it.

6. Sprinkle some powdered sugar onto your work surface. Rub the shortening on your hands, and then knead the paste together until you have a dough that is firm and smooth and not sticky.

7. Wrap in plastic wrap and place in a sealed plastic bag overnight to age and mature. Let come to room temperature before use.

Pro Tip

Nicholas Lodge
www.nicholaslodge.com

Gumpaste is very sensitive to air and can start to crack and dry out quickly. Always condition your gumpaste by kneading a little shortening into it before working with it. Keep gumpaste projects under a cup or under plastic to keep from drying out.

ROYAL ICING

Royal icing can be poured, piped, or frosted, depending on its consistency. It is used in a multitude of ways, from outlining and adding accents to cookies to delicate string work on cakes. I mostly use it for writing or piping details onto cakes. The key to royal icing is to not make it too stiff and always whip before using. Make sure you completely sift the powdered sugar to avoid getting sugar lumps in your piping tips. For the greatest amount of control when piping, small bags work better than large ones.

Ingredients:

8–12 oz/227–340 g confectioners' sugar, sifted

2 large egg whites

1. Weigh confectioners' sugar and sift.

2. Put egg whites into the bowl of a stand mixer with paddle attachment, and turn on low for a moment to break them up.

3. Slowly add sugar and turn the mixer up to medium.

4. Let whip until glossy, soft peaks form. If icing is too stiff, add a few drops of water and whip again. (A little water goes a long way.)

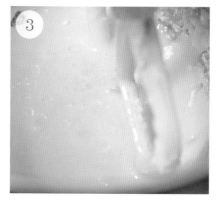

PIPING BASICS

Piping is a versatile technique that can be used in several ways. Depending on the type of tip you choose, you can use piping to create borders, patterns, textures, and lettering on your cakes. Both royal icing and buttercream can be used for piping.

PIPING BAGS

There are several options when it comes to piping bags. Your choice will depend on what you are planning to do. If you're going to be icing dozens of cupcakes or applying large amounts of buttercream to a cake, you will want to use a large piping bag. Choose a reusable bag that is flexible so that you don't have to squeeze very hard for the buttercream to come out easily and smoothly. A coated bag will make washing easy and prevent color staining of your bag.

Another type of bag you can use is a disposable one. Disposable piping bags are meant for onetime use and are great if you are working with multiple colors for a design or just need a bag for a quick job or a touch up. To fill the bags, I place them into a jar or cup, fold the top edge over, and spoon in the buttercream so I have both my hands free. Keep the back of the bag twisted tightly as you pipe to prevent the buttercream from squeezing out the back of the bag.

You can also make your own piping bag out of parchment paper. Here's how:

1. Start with a square of parchment paper.

2. You can fold a corner over and cut with the flat edge of a knife to form a triangle.

3. With the point facing you, take the right point, and fold it over until it matches up with the middle point.

4. Do the same with the left side.

5. Fold the points over, and then make two tears on either side of the center seam and fold down to keep the bag from unfolding.

6. Trim the tip off, fill with buttercream, roll down the edge, and pipe away!

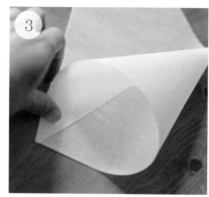

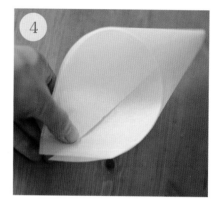

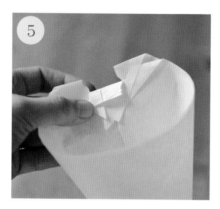

PIPING TIPS

A good set of tips is essential. Tips are available in both metal and plastic. Both work well. Whichever type you choose, make sure to wash them thoroughly after each use and allow to air dry completely before storing. Two of the most basic, yet versatile, tips are the star tip and the round tip, both of which are available in a number of different sizes.

STAR TIPS

Star tips are great for borders, scrollwork, simple flowers, stars, and shell borders.

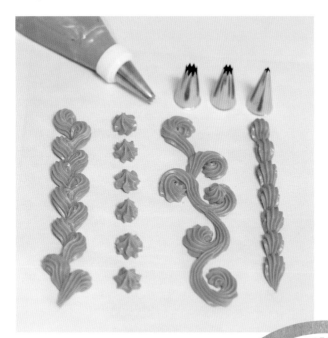

ROUND TIPS

Round tips are used for making dots, intricate scroll work, straight lines, borders, and lettering.

Baker's Secret

A coupler is a handy tool for piping that saves time and frosting. It is a small plastic adapter that is inserted into the piping bag and allows you to switch out tips on the same piping bag. It can be used with any type of bag.

Pro Tip

Corrie Rassmussin - Corrie's Cakes
www.facebook.com/CorrieCakes

Use a crusting buttercream for piping, but cut down on the amount of water called for. I use just a couple of tablespoons of water, as opposed to ¼–½ cup called for in most recipes. The only secret for neat and even piping is practice, practice, practice! Pipe borders, write out birthday messages, make scrolls. Try out different tips on the kitchen counter. Pipe out your design, and then just scrape it up and try again. You can also search for "piping templates" on the Internet and print them out. Slip them under some parchment, and practice your patterns to get better at hand control.

With just a few basic tips and a couple of different colors of frosting, you can begin creating complete designs and patterns. To make this floral vine, start by making a scroll design with a round tip. Then add some leaves with a leaf tip, and finish it off with some simple flowers made using a star tip.

  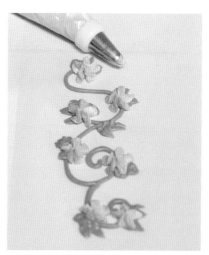

DECORATING A CAKE WITH PIPING

Start with a cake freshly frosted in buttercream and chilled.

1. Tint some crusting buttercream with avocado green food color, and mix until blended.

2. Fill a piping bag with a few spoonfuls of frosting, and twist the top of the bag.

3. Using a round tip, pipe some simple scroll work onto the side of your cake. You can always scrape the buttercream off if you make a mistake.

4. Use a star tip to create a shell border on the bottom edge of the cake.

5. With some pink frosting, pipe simple flower shapes. Fill in with a few dots.

6. Finish the top edge with a simple border using a round tip as shown.

Finish the design with a scroll design on top of the cake and a pretty gumpaste flower, or pipe on a message.

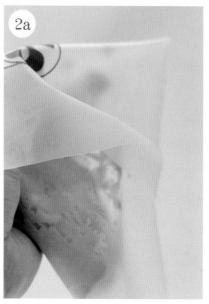
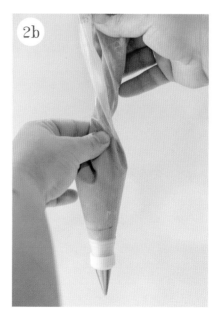

CHAPTER 2

CAKE PREPARATION

Preparing your cake is arguably the most important step in the decorating process and also the one that is the most overlooked. We all want to get to the fun part, the decorating, but the problem with not taking the time to properly prepare your cakes is that the final product will be marred with bumps, lumps, blowouts, and flaws that no amount of beautiful decorations will be able to fix or hide.

Trying to get sharp edges, clean lines, smooth fondant, and crisp designs was a constant struggle as a beginning decorator. I would look at those pretty cakes online and always wonder how they achieved such perfection. This chapter will focus on the preliminary work necessary to prepare your cake for a flawless finish.

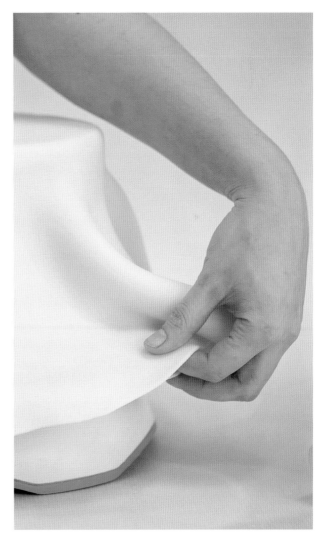

BAKING

I always bake my cakes the day before I decorate them. In one day, I shoot for getting the cakes baked, chilled, filled, and crumb coated. Then I refrigerate them overnight to allow them to settle and chill all the way through before decorating the next day. You can also bake one day, fill and chill the next, and decorate the third day. Butter is the crucial ingredient in cakes in relation to decorating because it gets firm when it is chilled. This is what allows you to trim off edges and tort (cut in half) cakes easily without them crumbling or falling apart. It is also almost impossible to neatly frost a freshly baked cake, and trying to carve an unchilled cake is a recipe for disaster.

Once the cakes are baked, I pull them out of the oven, place on a cookie rack, and immediately take a clean tea towel and gently press down the domed portion of the cakes. This does not hurt the cakes at all and actually makes the crumb denser (and results in less cake waste as well). I then allow them to cool. Small ones I will let cool for about 10 minutes before flipping over; larger ones might need to cool for 20 minutes before it is safe to flip. To flip the cake, I place the cooling rack over the pan, and with one hand over the rack and the other under the pan I flip the cake over and gently tap the back of the pan until the cake releases and comes out. Depending on your pan, you might need to use a knife to release the edges of your cake before flipping or use parchment in the bottom to aid in the release. I use a thin layer of vegetable shortening and a light dusting of flour to coat my pans.

While the cakes are in the refrigerator chilling, I make my buttercream. I use Swiss meringue buttercream (see recipe, page 34) on all of my cakes. The reason I like it is because it is fairly easy to make, spreads wonderfully, and allows me to get those super sharp edges. You can also use ganache (see recipe, page 39).

Baker's Secret

Go easy when greasing your cake pans. If you use too much vegetable shortening and flour to coat your pans, you will get a gooey, rough texture on the outside of your cakes, and your edges will not be crisp and clean.

STACKING CAKES

1. Place your cake on a turntable so you will have easy and smooth access all the way around. Begin by trimming off the dome.

2. Then tort—or split lengthwise—each layer. You can use either a special cutter called a cake leveler or a serrated bread knife. A shorter knife is better than one that reaches all the way across. Begin by making a small cut midway through the cake all the way around the outside. Slowly begin cutting into the cake right in the center. Make small sawing motions, letting the knife do the work. Continue the cut all the way around, staying in the center and turning the cake as you go. Keep your knife flat. Once you reach the middle, you are done. Do not be tempted to cut straight across. Your cut will be crooked, which means your entire cake will mostly likely end up crooked later.

3. Prepare a cardboard round that's the same diameter as the cake layers by putting a good-sized dollop of buttercream in the center and smoothing out to the edges.

Baker's Secret

Do not be tempted to overfill your layers with filling. The weight of your cake will squish it out and create bulges on the sides of your cake that are visible no matter how much of a dam you make.

4. Attach your first layer of cake topside down. Push the cake down until it meets the board. The buttercream will fill in any holes and "glue" it to the board. Fill your first layer with buttercream or other type of filling. If it is a liquidy filling, you may want to pipe in a dam of buttercream around the edge first to help hold the filling in.

5. Continue stacking and filling in this manner. I usually use two 2 in/5 cm cake layers that are cut in half, but other bakers may use three layers. How many you use is up to your preference. Trim off any pieces of cake that are extending past the cardboard so they do not poke through the buttercream layer. Some bakers even trim off a little cake all the way around to ensure the cleanest results.

6. Once the cakes are filled, and you have put on the top layer, apply a thin coat of buttercream to the entire outside of the cake to seal it. This is called the crumb coat because it prevents crumbs from getting into the decorative layer of your frosting. Place in the refrigerator or freezer until firm. I prefer to leave mine in the refrigerator overnight to chill through. After cakes are crumb coated, they will not dry out in the refrigerator.

ICING THE CAKE
TRADITIONAL TECHNIQUE

1. Once the cake is chilled, it's time to coat it in buttercream. Apply a nice thick coat of buttercream all the way around and on top of the cake.

2. For the sides, use your bench scraper and hold the end flat against the turntable and begin rotating and scraping the excess buttercream off little by little. (For frosting larger cakes, place your tier onto a cutting board or larger cake board and then onto the turntable so you have room to use the bench scraper.) It is important to keep the bench scraper straight up and down and wipe off the excess buttercream occasionally. Once you hit the cardboard base, you are done. Using an offset spatula, smooth the top edges. You should have a nice straight cake at this point, but it's not done yet.

3. Place the cake back in the refrigerator for 10 to 15 minutes to firm up again. The final step is to run some hot water over your bench scraper and give your layer one last go round, and then fill in any little holes or gaps and really clean up that edge with a small offset spatula. You now have a perfect cake that you can cover in fondant or decorate as is.

ICING SQUARE CAKES

1. To ice a square cake, trim, tort, fill, apply a crumb coat, and chill as usual. Ice the top of the cake, same as in the Traditional Technique on page 58.

2. Apply buttercream to the sides and then use your bench scraper to build up your corners and edges by applying buttercream to the edge of your scraper and then applying it onto the corners and then pulling away flat against the side of the cake. Once you have built up your corners and it looks pretty good, chill it until the buttercream is firm.

3. Use your bench scraper to scrape off the lumps and bumps and build up any low corners or spots with fresh buttercream. Use your level to check for even sides and straight corners. Then chill your cake again and give it a final going over with the bench scraper and small offset spatula as described on page 58.

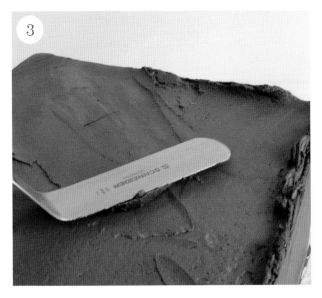

UPSIDE-DOWN TECHNIQUE

Start with a round or square cake that is completely chilled and crumb coated with buttercream for this method, which I learned from Jessica Harris (www.jessicakesblog.blogspot.com).

1. Begin by placing a piece of parchment paper onto a cardboard round or square that is larger than your cake by at least 4 in/10 cm on each side.

2. Spread at good dollop of buttercream onto your parchment and spread evenly into a flat ½-in-/1.25-cm-thick layer at least as wide as your cake.

3. Take the cake and carefully flip it over with flat hands on the sides of the cake (don't worry, it won't come apart) and place upside down onto the buttercream. Push the cake into the buttercream and use a level to make sure the cake is straight.

4. Once leveled, scrape off the excess buttercream from around the base.

5. Build up the buttercream in the same way as in the traditional method, page 58, using your bench scraper to get the sides perfectly straight.

6. Remember to keep your bench scraper straight up against the cake and continue removing excess buttercream until you hit the cardboard. Put in the refrigerator to chill again.

7. When you remove from the refrigerator, flip the cake back over. Place one hand over the cardboard on top and the other hand under the board on the bottom and quickly flip over in one movement. Remove the cardboard and peel off the parchment paper, and you will have a perfectly flat and sharp-edged cake. Place back in the refrigerator until you are ready to decorate or cover in fondant.

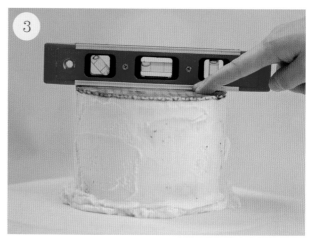

PANELING A CAKE WITH FONDANT OR MODELING CHOCOLATE

Another way to cover your cake with fondant is using the paneling method instead of trying to cover the cake in one piece. This technique is preferable if you want the sides to be a different color from the top, you want very sharp edges, or you want the seams to be visible for certain designs.

Paneling a cake in fondant or modeling chocolate is pretty straightforward. Tort and crumb coat your cake as usual. Then, roll out a piece of fondant or modeling chocolate for the top first.

1. Lay it on top of the cake.

2. Smooth.

3. Hold your blade straight up and down and make smooth cuts. Try not to make a sawing motion as this creates a jagged edge.

4. To calculate how much fondant you will need for the sides on a round cake, multiply π (3.14) by the diameter. This will give you the inches you need to roll out in length. Measure the height.

5. Cut a piece that is 1 in/2.5 cm taller than what you need.

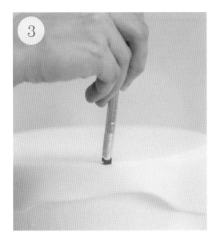

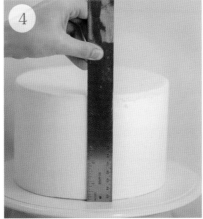

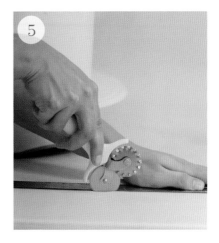

6. Roll the fondant onto a small rolling pin or piece of PVC, keeping the bottom edge of the fondant in line with the bottom of the pin.

7. With the fondant on the pin or pipe, begin wrapping it around the cake, pressing as you go to attach.

8. Fold the top bit of fondant over for now. Overlap the last bit and use a sharp knife or X-ACTO knife to cut through both layers of fondant.

9. Remove the excess and the bit underneath.

10. Rub the seams together.

11. Smooth.

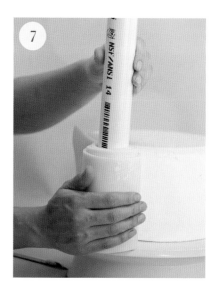

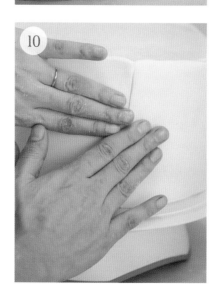

12. Trim off the top of the fondant with your sharp blade.

13. Use a little bit of vegetable oil to smooth. You can also use this technique for squares or odd shapes.

Baker's Secret

Clean your blade frequently to prevent sticking. Coat with a bit of vegetable shortening after cleaning to keep cuts smooth.

CHAPTER 3

ELEMENTS AND PRINCIPLES OF CAKE DESIGN

One of the advantages of having a background in graphic design and fine art is that I had the opportunity to learn the fundamentals of what makes something attractive and eye-catching. The principles of design used in graphic design and other artistic endeavors are just as important and applicable to cake design. Whether a cake looks good or not isn't just an accident or intuition, it's based on concrete knowledge. Basically, these principles and elements are tools you can use to create successful cake designs or troubleshoot ones that don't look quite right.

Just to be clear, there is a difference between bad execution and bad design. Some of the following cakes may not necessarily look unattractive, meaning that the cake decorating technique might be excellent, but these photos should help you understand the difference between a successful, attractive design and an unsuccessful one.

ELEMENTS

The elements of cake design are the visual pieces that make up your completed design. Elements tell the story of what your cake is trying to say. Is it fun, elegant, modern, or funky? The goal is to choose elements that complement and build upon each other, rather than clash, to create an effective, cohesive design.

Sometimes you might look at a cake you're working on and think that somehow it's just not coming together. How can you tell what to do to fix it?

Here are two examples of one cake. The one on the left demonstrates some misuse of elements, and the one on the right shows a dramatic improvement when the elements all work together. Study the following elements and principles. When something about your cake doesn't feel right, go through the list until you think you have discovered the specific problem, and then you'll know how to fix it.

In this cake, there are several conflicting design elements. The colors are not in the same scheme: some are pastel, some bright. The patterns are conflicting, and the elements are random, not repetitive. There is so much to look at that the eye isn't sure where to go.

In the revised design, the color scheme is based on the cube, and the colors, patterns, and shapes are repeated throughout the cake to give it visual unity. The typeface for the writing is bold and consistent with the other elements. The eye is led by colors and repeating shapes in the cake.

LINE AND PATTERN

Line refers to a mark on the surface of your cake. It may be thick or thin, create texture, repeat, or stand alone. The type of line you create will convey different feelings. Curved lines can feel elegant and sophisticated or natural. Straight lines are technical, modern, or masculine. Thick lines are strong and visually heavy. Thin lines are delicate, feminine, and light. Lines also give direction. Diagonal and vertical lines are energetic and move the eye, while horizontal lines elicit calm and peaceful feelings.

When using curved lines, make sure your design has a "flow," or you will subtract from the natural feeling of a curved line (left). If you are using straight lines, make sure they all have a beginning and a destination.

TEXTURE

There are two kinds of texture in cake design. There is actual surface texture created by adding three-dimensional surface quality to your cake, and then there is simulated texture that is done with color and appears to be textured, but is only two dimensional. Textures can be created randomly or with shapes that repeat and are small enough that, at first glance, the overall look is of texture, not individual shapes.

UNSUCCESSFUL DESIGN

Even when a texture is random, you should still consider flow and make your marks with intention. The photo (above) lacks purposeful flow in the texture. The sketch on the right shows how to correct this problem. Curve your marks to follow design components and keep your eye moving subliminally. Line is the most effective tool in guiding the eye, and texture is just another way to make a line.

COLOR

To use this critical element properly in cake design, you must first understand the basics of what color is and how to control it.

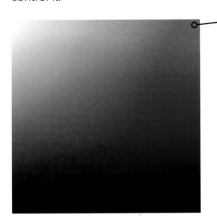

100 percent red hue

Hue

Hue refers to a color in its purest state without any dark or light pigments added. Hue is represented below by the color wheel. Using pure color creates a look that is high energy, playful, and really draws the eye. Using 100 percent hue in your designs will also seem cartoonish or childlike, since 100 percent hue does not exist in nature. You will also find that placing two 100 percent hues that are complementary (red/blue) and that are the same value (see below) will "vibrate" and feel very uncomfortable to the eye.

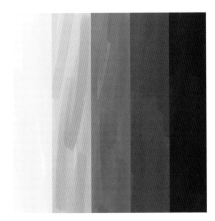

Value

Value refers to how light or dark a color is. Adding white to a color is called a *tint* and creates pastel colors. A tint tends to read as soft, pretty, calm, or feminine. Adding black or colors that have black in them is called a *shade*. Shades can look masculine, heavy feeling, and dramatic. When adding dark color to lighter colors (yellow, orange), a small amount makes a big difference. The darker your hue (blue, purple), the more dark color you will have to add to have an impact. Adding grey (white with a touch of black) will create a muted or neutral color scheme, and this is called a *tone*. A tone makes a full saturation color seem more realistic to our eye because no color found in nature is full saturation. There are always highlights and lowlights that tone down the color to our eye.

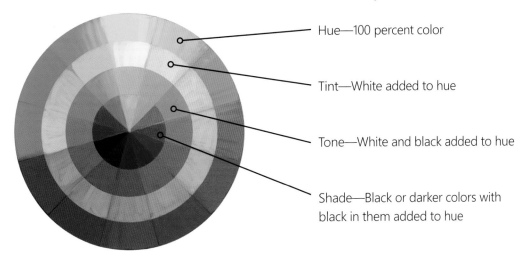

Hue—100 percent color

Tint—White added to hue

Tone—White and black added to hue

Shade—Black or darker colors with black in them added to hue

Color Schemes

Primary Colors
The base from which all colors are made

Secondary Colors
Made by mixing two primary colors

Baker's Secret

Choose the color palette for your cake early in the design planning process. Pick a main color, secondary color, and accent colors if you plan to use any.

Complementary
Opposite from each other on the wheel; look good together

Analogous
Colors that are next to each other on the color wheel

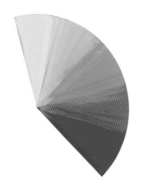

Split Complementary
Two analogous colors and one complementary color

VISUAL CONTRAST

Contrast is the difference between color (hue) or value (dark to light) in relationship to each other. For instance, lavender and white have a medium contrast because there is a fairly large difference between white and lavender value, so the colors are easier to differentiate. However, lavender and light green have a very similar value, even though the hue is different. When the eye cannot differentiate between colors well (low contrast), the colors become muddled and confused and not as pleasing to the eye.

When you have no choice but to use a color scheme that has little value difference, you must try and incorporate a neutral color like black or white into the mix to separate similar values from each other. Note how much better the designs look in the middle and on the right, using white, than the one on the left. Similar playful shapes and placement still get the design concept across without sacrificing contrast.

SHAPE

Shapes are the areas created by lines, value, texture, or the empty spaces between elements. Shape is two dimensional. Your choice of shape can convey different ideas or feelings. Geometric shapes are precise, mathematical, masculine and, depending on color, can be sophisticated or cartoonlike. Natural shapes are those usually found in nature, such as flowers, leaves, curves, and free-flowing piping. Natural shapes are soft, organic, and feminine. Nonrepresentational shapes can be dynamic or subdued. Sharp edges create drama and energy, while soft shapes are calm and more playful. When shapes are not clearly defined, the cake design can become confusing.

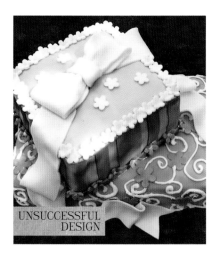

When creating geometric shapes, make sure your shapes are clean with straight edges. Squares that aren't quite square or stripes that look more like wet noodles will detract from the overall look of a cake. The photo on the top left uses plenty of shapes, but they are not cleanly defined by sharp lines or value as they are in the sketch.

Be careful about mixing geometric and organic shapes. It can be done, as the photo to the right shows, but requires forethought and intention. It can be easy to start adding on more and more shapes because things don't look "right," but that can get you into a deeper mess. Keep your organic shapes sharp so that what they are is clear. Sketching really helps with this part of the design process.

The bottom left photo has hand-painted shapes, but they are hard to see because there are no defined areas. Everything becomes visually confused. The sketch, middle, shows the corrected design. On the right is another example of a successful design.

SIZE

Size refers to the proportion of one thing in relation to another. A marble is small compared to a baseball, but a baseball is small compared to a basketball. Considering proportions in how elements relate to each other will create a more pleasing composition.

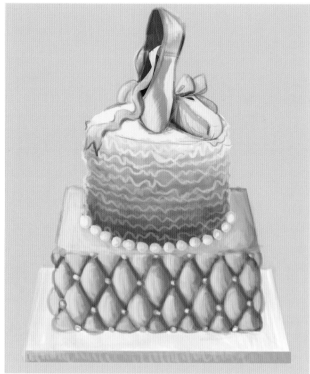

In general, a cake is shaped like a pyramid. The base layer is the largest part, and elements get lighter and smaller as you move upwards. When something breaks this law, it can feel odd to the eye (left). Similarly, when some elements are out of proportion to their surrounding elements, they can feel out of balance and too visually heavy for the design.

In this cake, the base appears heavier and decorative elements get lighter and smaller as you move up the cake. The final effect is very visually pleasing.

DIRECTION

Direction is the invisible path your eye takes when looking at a composition. Your eye wants to move naturally from left to right and from top to bottom (how we read English). Your eye will notice darker and brighter elements first and then move on down to lighter, more muted elements. Use colors, contrast, and shapes to lead the eye around a composition.

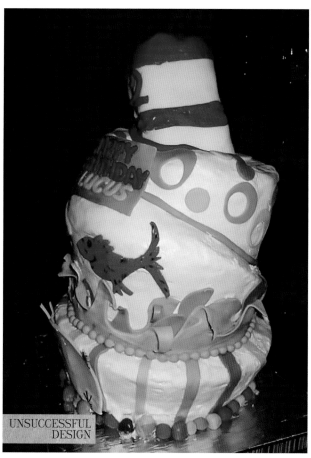

UNSUCCESSFUL DESIGN

When a cake design has a lot of elements in it, it can easily become too busy and jumbled (upper left). Because the eye naturally begins at the top of a design, you can use the color or another element that is at the top of the cake to lead the eye through a busy design subconsciously as the sketch (left), shows. For the cake on the top left, the eye gets stuck, and the design doesn't make sense.

PRINCIPLES

The principles of cake design are the ways that you use the elements to help you create a successful composition. Principles impact how you "feel" about a cake when you look at it. It is hard to point out just one principle in a design; it is more about how all the principles work together. When you sketch a design, it's a good idea to go through the list of principles and see if your design is lacking in any of the areas.

FOCAL POINT

What does your eye go to first? A focal point is created with contrast, color, placement, or just by being different from everything else in the design. The greater the difference, the stronger the focal point. A strong focal point makes you stop and notice something because it stands out. If there is no focal point, a cake will lack interest, and the viewer will not know where to look.

One way to make something a focal point is to make it different from everything else in the design. This also helps to draw the eye if you want the focal point not to be at the top. In the photo, right, the monogram is the focal point and then flowers, repetitive colors, textures, and patterns lead the eye down the cake design and back to the focal point. In the photo on the left, the dark leaves are the unintentional focal point, which is odd. The sketch in the center shows this problem corrected.

BALANCE

Visual balance in cake design is the equal distribution of elements and visual weight in the design. Imagine an invisible line down the center of your cake. To have a balanced design you need to have equal visual weight on each side of the line. The rule is, if you do something in one place, whether it is a color, an element, or even an empty space, you need to do the same thing in another place on the other side of the line.

Symmetrical Designs

A symmetrical design has the same elements on one side of a cake as on the other. This type of design is usually the choice for cakes that have prominent textures, patterns, or strong use of geometric shapes. Symmetrical does not always mean boring, but there is less visual energy than in an asymmetrical design.

UNSUCCESSFUL DESIGN

Symmetrical designs are very visually appealing and a great design option for cakes that have a lot of detail and texture. The photo on the left uses a symmetrical design in some areas, but the flowers and black dots are not evenly placed and spaced. If you are going to be symmetrical, be consistent. Use of repetitive elements creates interest, while keeping things symmetrical creates an orderly and sophisticated look, as illustrated in the corrected cake in the sketch on the right.

Equal focal points

UNSUCCESSFUL
DESIGN

Asymmetrical Designs

Asymmetrical designs are more dynamic and energetic. Elements are off center and force your eye to move around the cake design. The photo on the far left shows an almost asymmetrical design, but the flowers are too close to the same level, so the design seems boring and odd. The further an element is away from the center point of the cake, the stronger the opposing element will have to be to balance it out, as the corrected sketch on the near left shows.

Radial Balance

Elements radiate from a central focal point, and weight is symmetrically balanced.

Crystallographic Balance

Elements repeating in a pattern create equal visual weight all over the design. Geometric patterns are a good example of this.

Asymmetrical designs are still balanced, though not necessarily by the same element. For example, you can balance out a large flower in the upper right of a cake with a large amount of empty space in the lower right. Objects have more visual weight than empty space, so you see that first and then move to large open spaces. A large amount of space has the same amount of weight visually as a colorful flower.

VISUAL WEIGHT

Where an element is placed will determine how you will need to balance it out. Remember that the "heavier" an object is, the more visual pull it has. The further from the center line an element is placed, the more visual weight it has. You can use this to your advantage by placing objects with more visual weight in areas that you want the eye to go to first, second, third, and so on.

Size

Large objects feel heavier than smaller objects. Use larger objects to balance out other areas of texture or empty space.

Texture

Areas with more texture feel visually heavier than empty spaces. You can use texture to balance out heavier elements or to give interest to empty spaces.

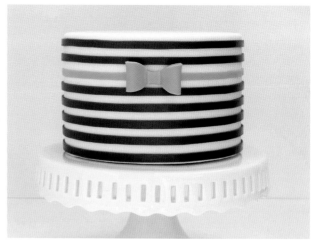

Saturation

Bright colors will attract your eyes more than subdued colors. You can use bright colors to lead your eye around a design or to balance out large empty spaces or busy patterns.

Value and Contrast

Darker elements feel heavier than lighter elements and will attract your eyes first. The more contrast between elements, the heavier they will feel.

Isolation

Elements that are isolated stand out visually because they are all alone. This can look odd, or it can be dynamic, depending on how you use it. Isolation works best with focal points.

Repetition

Multiple or repeated small elements can balance out the weight of one large object.

HARMONY

All the elements complement each other and give each other strength, creating one beautiful, cohesive message. The main focal point is clear, the supporting elements are interesting, the colors feel right. Methods of achieving harmony in a design fall into four categories.

Proximity
Elements that are close to each other appear as a whole, rather than as separate pieces.

Alignment
Lining up the edges of elements helps the eye to sub-consciously group elements together. You can align by the center line, or by the top or bottom edge of objects.

Harmonious Repetition
Grouping elements that are similar—such as lines, textures, or patterns—helps them look as if they are part of a whole.

Continuation

When you line up elements in an orderly way, your eye naturally follows them like stepping stones, making the design appear as one seamless piece.

VARIETY

Variety without harmony can look erratic and odd, but the good kind of variety can add dimension and life to your cake design. A good rule of thumb is to add variety to elements that are already similar (patterns, texture, shapes, lines, color).

Patterns
Mixing patterns can create a dynamic design, but the colors and other elements must maintain a complementary theme in order for the design to be successful.

Texture
Varying textures on a cake design can create beautiful results, but make sure your textures match in either color or theme.

Once you begin to understand simple concepts in color and design, you will begin to see patterns everywhere, from furniture to fabric to nature. Being able to recognize elements all around you will enable you to implement them into your own designs and greatly increase your creative options.

Color

Mixing up the hue, value, and saturation can create interest, but make sure your colors, hues, and value still work together, following the color wheel rules.

Shape

By varying size and orientation, you can create more energy, movement, and interest.

Lines

Varying the line width, value, color, length, and shape can add real interest, especially to piping.

CHAPTER 4
TEXTURES AND FINISHES

While cakes with basic colors on a flat surface of buttercream or fondant can look fine, adding texture, more intricate coloring, or a specialty finish can really up the "wow" factor and elevate a cake from ordinary to extraordinary. Here are a few examples of popular finishes, textures, and coloring effects, and how to achieve them. Keep in mind there is often more than one way to create a special effect. Experiment and learn what works best for the look you want to create.

TEXTURING BUTTERCREAM

The simplest way to add texture to a cake is to create it in the frosting itself. This rustic waves texture looks deceptively simple, but it takes a few key steps to get a finished look that's clean and pretty and not amateurish.

1. Always begin with a cleanly frosted cake. I use the Crusting Buttercream (see recipe, page 33) for this type of cake because, just as its name says, the buttercream crusts over and sets, so your design will not get ruined if it is accidentally touched.

2. Use a small offset spatula to apply small amounts of buttercream to the surface of your chilled and prepped cake. Make a small "C" motion as you apply. Overlap each new layer.

Finish with a pretty gumpaste flower or decorate with fresh flowers.

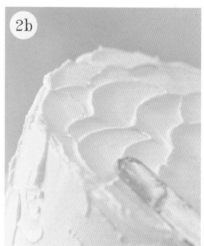

CHAPTER 5
MODELED FIGURES

Modeled figures of people, animals, or other creatures are an integral part of many specialty cake designs. The first step in making figures is always a sketch. Drawing out the figure you plan to create will help you understand all the different elements of the design and the materials needed. It will also help you visualize the process of building your figure piece by piece.

Next, decide what you'll use to make your figure. Modeling chocolate, fondant, or gumpaste are all suitable mediums for figures. If your figure is going to be standing or there are skinny pieces (arms, legs, etc.), you will probably need internal supports to maintain shape and to keep the figure from collapsing.

One of the first mistakes I ever made as a beginner was not putting an internal structure in my cake toppers. Most toppers, because they are small, can be managed with just a single internal support. One of the most common internal supports is a wooden skewer, but I prefer lollipop or cake pop sticks. They are slightly flexible, made of a food-safe paper, and will not cause injury if someone accidentally bites into it. This is especially important to consider when making cakes for kids. Always let people know when there are inedible supports in your toppers or cakes.

An internal support is an important step in making sure your fondant, gumpaste, or modeling chocolate stays put. These materials are inclined to settle, and that can make figures very short and fat very quickly. Just about 99 percent of my cake toppers are made by inserting a lollipop stick into a foam block and building upon it. Sometimes I add anodized wire (coated wire used in jewelry making) for arms or extended legs. I prefer to work with fondant that has tylose powder added to it, but other cake artists prefer modeling chocolate. Experiment and find what works best for you. There is no wrong way to do something unless it is not working.

Generally, it's best to work on figures from the bottom up or the center out, and let each element dry before going on to the next step. I usually start with the body and build it up around the support structure. Once that is dry, I add on legs and arms and, last, the head or higher elements.

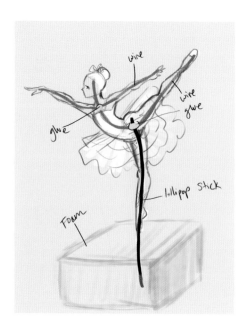

Ballerina topper made with wire support has modeling chocolate for the body and fondant for the head, shoes, and tutu top. I made the ruffled tutu skirt out of Sugar Dress for a realistic and natural-fabric look.

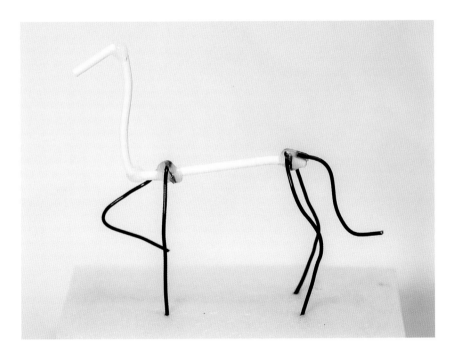

This horse topper uses a lollipop stick bent to shape and wires for legs and tail. The outer body of the horse is modeling chocolate with accents of petal dusts.

PRO PROJECT: FAIRY

This fairy is highly detailed and somewhat complex, but not too difficult to make if you follow the directions step by step.

Equipment:

Modeling tools

X-ACTO knife

Gum glue

Brush

Ball tools

Cake pop sticks

24-gauge floral wire

Face mold

Small leaf cutter

Small flower cutter

Edible Supplies:

Fondant, with tylose powder: ivory, dark green, light green, yellow, and black

Food coloring

Wafer paper

BODY

Start by constructing the fairy's body using the fairy template (see page 219). Roll out a ball of ivory fondant into a long snake to make a leg, using the template for reference.

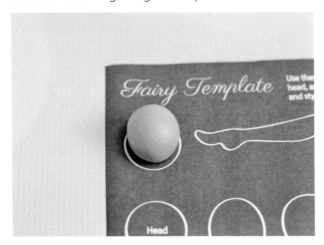
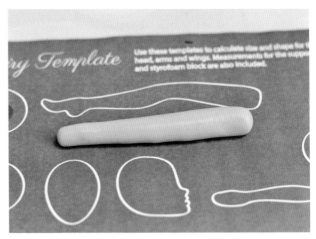

Use your finger to thin out the ankle area. Then indent an area for the bottom of the foot, and shape the heel and toe area. Pinch the toe area flat.

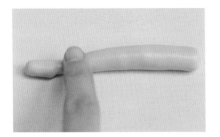
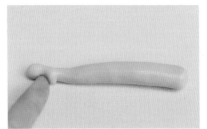
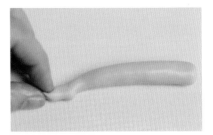

Pinch the middle of the leg with your fingers to create the upper calf area and thigh. Use the template to get the shape just right.

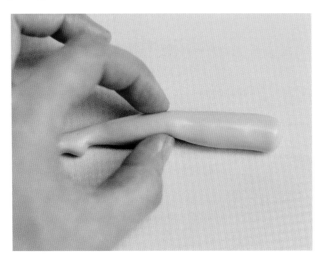
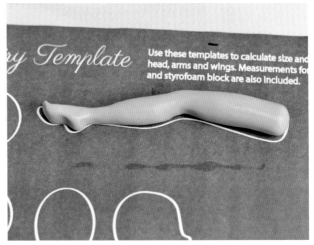

Pinch a spot right at the bend in the knee to give the kneecap a bit of definition.

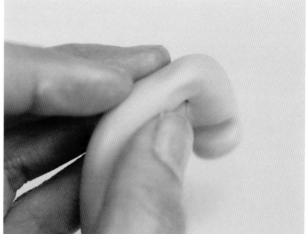

Push a cake pop stick into a foam block that's tall enough for the fairy's legs to dangle from without touching the ground. My blocks were not quite tall enough, so I taped two together.

Place the leg onto the block and wrap the end around the cake pop stick to hold it in place. Make another leg the same way as the first and wrap it around the stick in the same fashion. Glue the legs together with a bit of gum glue to keep them in place. Check the legs to make sure they are the same length.

Roll out another ball of your ivory fondant using your body template for reference. Use your finger to thin out the waist and neck. Use the template as a guide to make sure your proportions are correct. Bodies tend to get wider as you work on them so make your body skinnier than you think it should be.

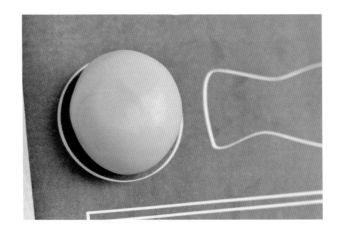

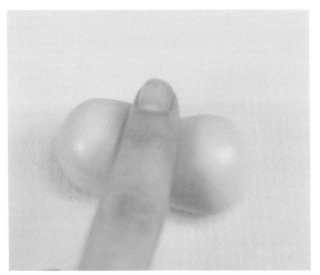

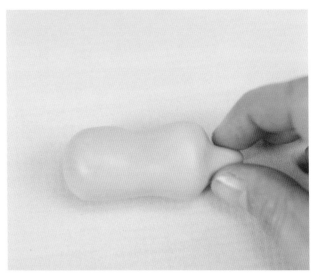

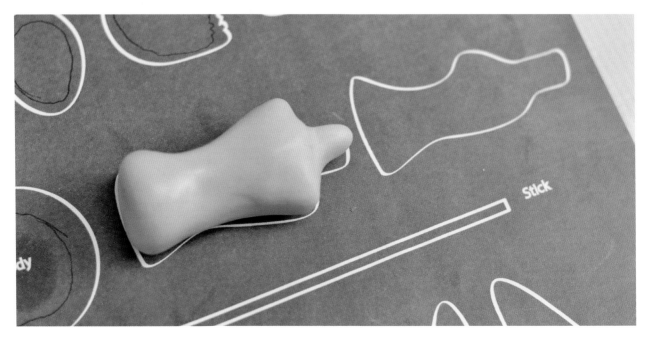

To make the wings, place two pieces of the wafer paper over your template and trace the outline of the wings. Dip two pieces of floral wire into the water and insert them in between the wings and press down. Wafer paper is very sensitive to water and will become sticky with just a small amount.

Cut out the wings and seal the edges of the wings with a brush and small amounts of water.

Trim the wire to a quarter inch and insert the wings into the back of the fairy.

CHAPTER 6

SUGAR FLOWERS

Sugar flowers provide endless possibilities for beautiful cakes. The advantage of using sugar flowers—besides being edible—is that you can get the exact color and shape that you want for your design, something not always possible using real flowers. I make my sugar flowers far in advance during my downtime. (I actually find it relaxing.)

The following are a few of my favorite types of sugar flowers to make. Some require molds; some do not. Learning to make a few sugar flowers with confidence will be a valuable addition to your cake decorating repertoire and a skill you will turn to again and again for creating lovely, memorable cakes.

SIMPLE FLOWERS, LEAVES, AND BERRIES

Filler flowers are a key part of any floral design. They are used to fill out an arrangement of larger flowers, and they also add texture, balance, and interest to the cake. Filler flowers can be made in bulk and stored. Once made, sugar flowers can be stored in an airtight container (out of the sun) for up to three months. If you make them in white, then you can just take out a few whenever you need to use them and dust with the appropriate color for your design.

Equipment Needed:

Small rolling pin or pasta machine

Floral wires

Floral stamens

Needle-nose pliers

Hydrangea cutter

Teardrop cutters

Large daisy cutter

Plastic wrap

Plastic cups

Brush for petal dust

Brush for gum glue

Petal impression molds (optional)

Leaf impression molds

Foam pads (soft and firm)

Large and medium ball tools

Toothpicks

Floral tape

DIY flower holder

DIY spoon petal holder

Modeling tool

Pointed modeling tool

Powdered sugar sifter

Edible Supplies:

Gumpaste

Gum glue

Petal dust (dark and light green, pink, red, green)

Food color (yellow, ivory, green, pink, black, purple)

Corn syrup

Grain alcohol (such as vodka)

GUMPASTE 101

Gumpaste is the medium used to make the sugar flowers and leaves shown here. It can be rolled thin and left to dry to a firmness that feels much like porcelain. Dried petals and flowers can be dusted and colored pretty much any way you can imagine. Working with gumpaste does take practice, though and can be a little frustrating at first. I hope these tips and tricks will help take the mystery out of gumpaste, and soon you'll be making flowers, leaves, and more with ease.

When working with gumpaste, always take it out of the refrigerator ahead of time so it can come to room temperature. When you first break off a piece, it will be very dry and crumbly. You will need to condition the paste by kneading in some vegetable shortening to moisten it before each use. If you notice your gumpaste cracking, knead in more shortening.

When working on flowers or other gumpaste projects, keep the extra paste you're not currently using covered with a plastic cup or a piece of plastic wrap to prevent it from drying out. (It dries out very quickly and is then difficult to work with.) After gumpaste projects are completely dry, you can dust them with powdered food colors called petal dust or you can airbrush them.

Always steam your finished flowers by holding them in front of an iron or steamer, or lightly spray them with a little water to seal in the color and bring them to life. If you don't do this, the colors will seem a bit dry, dull, and lifeless.

Gumpaste projects can be made days, weeks, or months in advance. Store them in an airtight container for future use. If your gumpaste is colored, be sure to keep the containers out of the sun to prevent fading.

SIMPLE HYDRANGEA

Buds and Centers

Start by making the centers of the flower and the buds. The technique is the same for both. Use a small ball of white gumpaste for the buds and balls of green or yellow gumpaste that are about half the size of the ones for the buds to make the centers. Take a piece of floral wire and bend over the tip with your needle-nose pliers—this helps the gumpaste ball attach and stay put. Dip the wire in a bit of gum glue and insert into one of the balls of gumpaste. Thin the base around the wire to secure it. Use your modeling tool to create a cross in the top. Place these on your egg foam to dry, or stick them into a foam block.

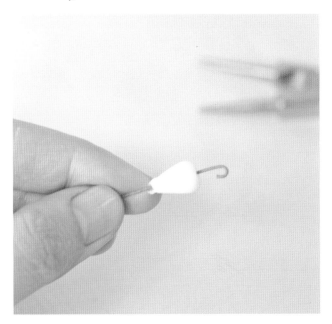

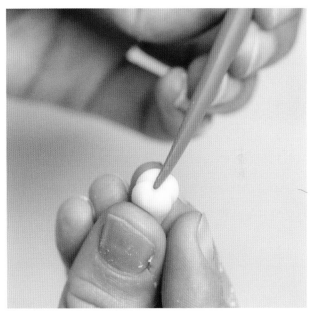

Hydrangea Flowers

To make the petals, use gumpaste that you have already conditioned, and roll it out using a pasta maker or rolling pin (see Baker's Secret on page 132). Use the hydrangea cutter to cut out two or three flower shapes. (Remember to store the rest of the gumpaste under plastic wrap so it does not dry out.) Thin your piece of gumpaste on a firm floral pad with a large ball tool. Press your cut piece into a mold to create the lines and textures of the petals. If you do not have a petal mold, you can use a Dresden tool to create lines in your petals. Start from the center and pull out towards the tips of the petals. Take one of your flower centers and thread the petals over the wire and onto the center ball, securing with a touch of gum glue.

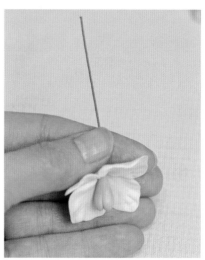

Thread the wire through your egg foam, and let the foam cup the shape of the petals while they dry. I put the egg foam on top of the wire rack to make room for the wires as I thread them through. After the petals are dry, dust them with a little color. Popular choices are yellow, blue, pink, or green.

Then use the medium ball tool to pull the petals towards the center. Begin at the tips, and with gentle pressure, pull towards the center to curl the petal. Dip a floral wire into the gum glue and thread into your petal. Place on the DIY spoon petal holder to dry overnight before dusting and assembling.

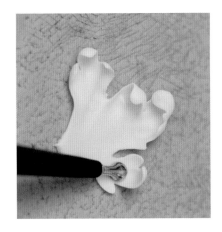
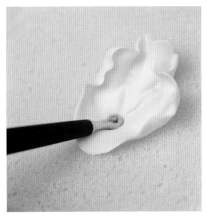

Repeat the same process with your medium and large petals except, during the curling of the petals, place them onto the soft foam pad. This will make deeper ridges and a more ruffled petal. (Make two to four medium and two to four large).

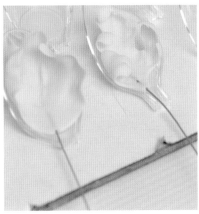

To assemble the flowers, hold a few flower stamens in your left hand and bend in half. Wrap a piece of floral wire around the stamens and twist to secure. Make a few of these to have on hand as you assemble your flowers. Begin attaching your petals, starting with the smallest. Depending on the size of the flower you want to make, attach two to three petals at this step. Twist the wires around the main wire as you add each petal to secure it. Then attach the medium and large petals.

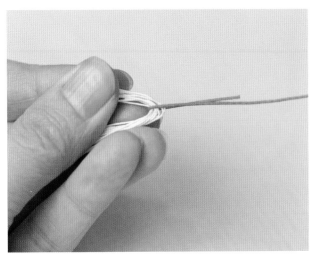

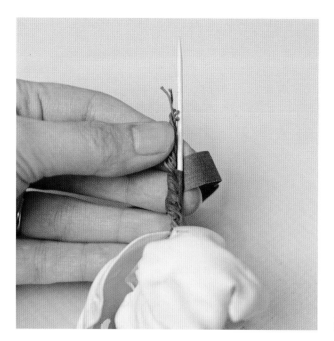 

After you have attached all your petals, align a toothpick with the wires and wrap with floral tape to secure. The toothpick should be longer than the wires so that you can easily insert your flower bunches into a cake while keeping your wire separate from the cake. I like to hold my flowers with needle-nose pliers while I insert them into the cake so I can minimize damage to petals while still keeping a firm grip on the stem.

Once dry, use a small fluffy brush to dust the edges of the outer petals with pink. For the small petals, I like to dust the tips and the ends so that, when the flower is assembled, I have color in the center.

DAHLIA

This flower makes a great focal point all by itself or with an arrangement of filler flowers. The petals look complicated but are actually quite simple to create. To make this flower larger, you simply add more rows of petals.

Begin by creating the center. Take a small 1 in/2.5 cm ball of green gumpaste and thread it onto a hooked wire. Take a slightly larger piece of green gumpaste and press it into the sifter to create a flower center texture. Use a modeling tool to texture the piece further. Attach this to your small ball of paste with a bit of gum glue. Turn upside down on your egg foam and let dry overnight.

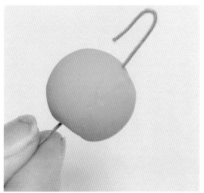
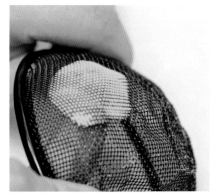
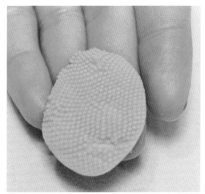

Roll out some pink gumpaste. Using your large daisy cutter, cut out a piece of paste. Thin the edges with your large ball tool.

Apply a bit of gum glue to the dried center and thread the wire through the middle of the petals and wrap around the dahlia center until they almost touch. Continue this way with four more petal layers.

 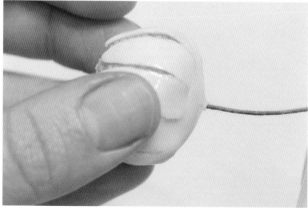

Roll out more pink gumpaste and cut out a few small teardrops. Work on one petal at a time and keep the others covered with plastic wrap while you work so they do not dry out. Thin the edges of the petals with your large ball tool and your firm foam pad. Roll into a cone and attach to your center with a little gum glue. Continue until your first row is finished. For the next two to three rows, you will use your large teardrop cutter. Continue making cones and attaching to your center until the flower is as large as you wish.

When you are finished, your flower should look slightly domed. Place on your egg foam to dry overnight. After it is dry, you can attach a toothpick to the back by inserting it slightly into the center alongside the wire and then securing with floral tape. This will help keep your flower secure when you attach it to your cake. Finish your flower by dusting with some pink petal dust. I dust the center more than the outer petals, keeping the dust mostly inside the cones.

Experiment with other colors and petal shapes of dahlia. They come in so many styles, but the basic concept is the same. Some petals are actually curved and pointed, others are more textured, and some are very long and thin. Look at gardening books, catalogs, and online for other color combinations.

CHAPTER 7

CELEBRATION CAKES

Celebration cakes are the centerpiece of any event. Whether it's a small family birthday party or a lavish wedding, no party is complete without the cake. What follows are the directions for two different celebration cakes. The techniques used can be applied to many other kinds of stacked cake designs. As with all my projects, I begin my cake design with a sketch. During client consultations or brain storming sessions, I will just sketch loosely on a pad of paper and make notes to myself. I don't focus too much on perfection here, just on getting my idea down. After I have my idea, I refine the image on the computer using a software program, some templates I made, and a tablet with stylus to mimic the feel of drawing on paper. Refining your sketch on old-fashioned paper with colored pencils works great too. At this stage, I make note of how big the tiers are, how many servings each tier provides, if elements are edible or not, and the flavors of each tier. This saves time and gives me peace of mind later when I'm trying to remember if those were sugar flowers or fresh flowers on the cake.

Baker's Secret

I offer a free digital cake-sketching class online through a website called cakefu.com. I go over the basics of using my cake templates (available for purchase) and how to bring your cake sketches to the next level by incorporating professional cake sketches. www.cakefu.com/masters-series/liz-marek-71

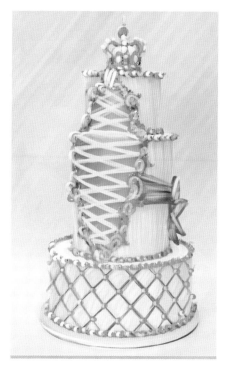

GETTING STARTED

PERFECT CAKE BOARDS

Every cake needs a cake board (unless you have a special plate or tray that you plan to put your cake on). This rounds out the presentation and provides a clean canvas for the cake to be presented on. I use pressboard, but cake drums or poster board will also work. A cake board should be at least 2 in/5 cm larger than the measurements of the bottom tier of the cake. (It may be even larger if there will be decorations or lettering on the board.)

Cut four small squares of poster board or cardboard and attach them to the bottom of your board using a glue gun. These "feet" allow you to slip your fingers under the board easily when you need to move your cake after it is decorated. Apply a thin layer of white shortening over the top of the board. Roll out a piece of fondant and smooth it over the board. Trim off the excess with a blade. Glue a ribbon around the edge to finish it off in a color that will go with your cake colors. Your board is now ready for its cake.

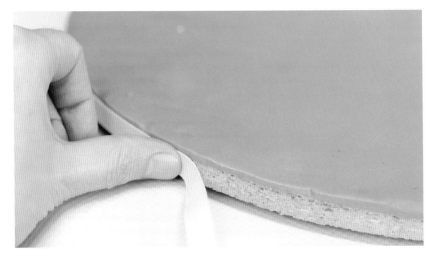

SUPPORTING TIERS

Whenever you stack one layer of a cake on top of another, you will need to support the weight of the upper layer and all the additional tiers stacked on top of that. Depending on how many tiers you stack, there can be quite a bit of weight on the bottom tier. Without supports, your cake would literally crumble under the weight. I like to use fat drinking straws to support my tiers. I purchase these at my local restaurant supply store. Some people use bubble straws and others use wooden dowels or Poly-Dowels (plastic dowels that look like really thick straws but can be cut easily). Whatever kind you choose, make sure they are strong enough and that you use enough of them to support the weight of your stacked tiers. The guide shown here will help you determine how many supports you need per tier and where to place them. This guide is based on fat straws; you may need more or fewer depending on the type of supports you use. After your cake is covered with buttercream and fondant, insert a support into the center of the cake, and mark with your finger or a pen where the top of the cake is. Use this as your guide to cut all the other supports to the same height. This will ensure your cake is level and straight. Remove the test support with your fingers or needle-nose pliers. If you need help visualizing where your supports should go, you can use a cake pan that is the same size as the tier above. Center it on the cake tier and lightly trace a guideline with a modeling tool.

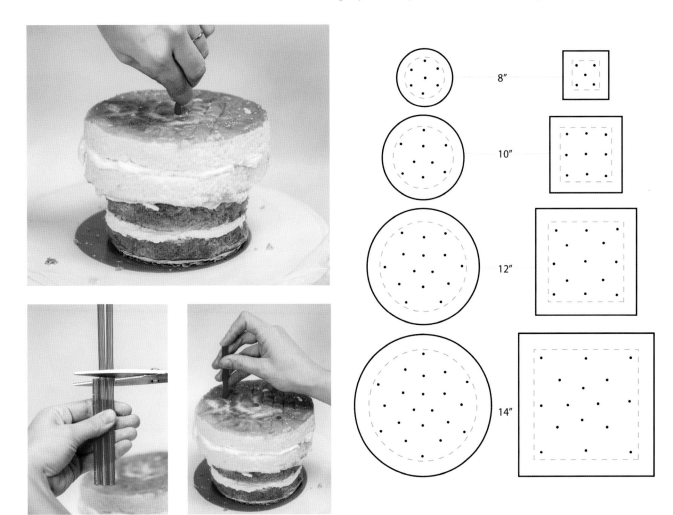

BLACKBERRY RUFFLE CAKE

This festive ruffle cake is so pretty, you won't want to cut into it. It's perfect for a rustic wedding.

Supplies:

White fondant with tylose, 2
batches

Pasta machine

X-ACTO knife

Ball tool

Foam pad

Gum glue

Needle-nose pliers

Straws

Toothpicks

Sugar flowers, berries, leaves, and
filler flowers from Chapter 6

Cakes (torted, filled, frosted,
and covered in fondant):
Two 10 in/25 cm
Two 8 in/21.25
One 6 in/15 cm
Two 4 in/10 cm

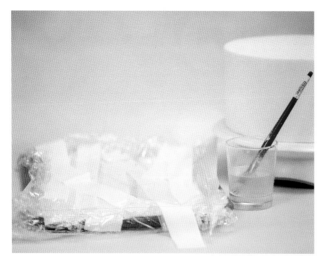

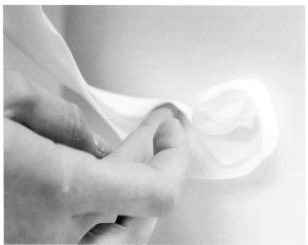

Prepare your cakes for decorating as instructed in Chapter 2. I did not make a cake board for this cake because I wanted to display it on a platter instead. If you prefer a cake board, you can prep one that is 12 in/30 cm in diameter.

Roll out a small amount of fondant with a rolling pin until thin enough to roll through the pasta machine. Roll to a setting of 4. If you do not have a pasta machine, roll fondant out by hand with a small rolling pin to about 1/16 in/1.6 mm thick, or about as thin as you can get it without tearing. Thinner fondant will result in more delicate looking ruffles. Cut into 1.5-in-/3.75-cm-wide strips, and store under plastic wrap until you use them.

Paint some gum glue onto the surface of the 10-in/25-cm tier. Fold one strip of fondant over lengthwise. Begin making your first large rosette. Start in the center. Use your finger to press the folded fondant into the cake as you go. Continue in this fashion until you have formed the entire rosette.

Support the rosette's ruffles with toothpicks until they dry. Make another rosette in the same way on the back of the cake. Then make one between each of the two roses for a total of four equally spaced rosettes going around the cake.

Take another folded strip of fondant and attach to the cake in the shape of a V. Add additional fondant V's starting at the bottom and working your way towards the top of the cake as shown. Fill in the gaps between the roses and the V by loosely rolling a folded fondant strip into a rosette. Place into the gap. Use toothpicks to support the ruffles as they dry.

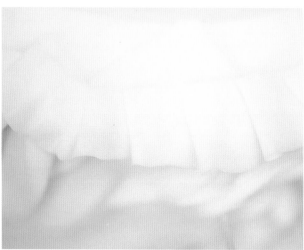

Insert nine straws, cut to equal length, into your bottom tier. Place the 8-in/20-cm tier on top of the 10 in/25 cm. Next, create some thin ruffles to finish the top of the 10-in/25-cm tier. Begin with your fondant rolled to a setting of 4. Cut into strips about ½ in/1.25 cm wide. Gather the strip to create a ruffle as pictured. Lay the gathered strip on the outside edge of the tier to be ruffled. Attach with a bit of water. Work your way all the way around, and then continue on with two more rows. Once you get the final row down, use your modeling tool to push the edge down flat and then to make small lines to create a tufted, ruffled look.

Baker's Secret

You don't have to use a pasta machine for this cake, but it makes things go a lot faster. A pasta machine will allow you to roll out a lot of fondant at once that is the same thickness. If you do not have a pasta machine, you will need to roll out the fondant as thin as you can without tearing it.

Place five straws in the top of the 8-in/20-cm tier. Place your 6-in/15-cm tier on top of the 8-in/20-cm tier. Finish the bottom edge of the 6-in/15-cm tier with a simple row of ruffles. Use a modeling tool to create some tufted lines around the base. Place three straws in the 6-in/15-cm tier to support the final 4-in/10-cm tier. Take your 4-in/10-cm tier (make sure it is chilled firm) and place it upside down on an upside-down 4-in/10-cm round cake pan. Don't worry, this won't cause any damage to the layer. Coat the tier in a little water to make the fondant tacky. Create some more ruffles in the same manner as above. Begin attaching the ruffles around the base of the tier as pictured.

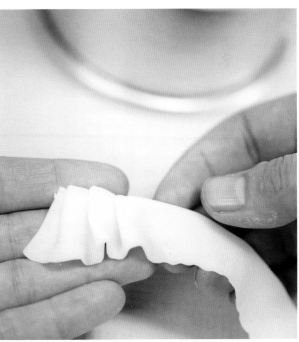

Continue attaching ruffles, slightly overlapping the previous row until you have the entire tier covered. Grasp the cake pan with one hand, sandwich the tier between the pan and your other hand, and flip back over carefully. Place the finished cake on top of the 6-in/15-cm tier.

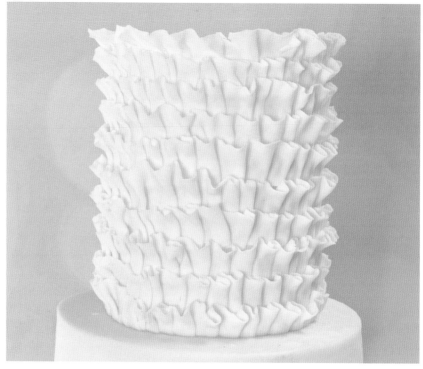

PLACING FLOWERS

Now it's time to place the flower arrangements on the cake. Begin by inserting a large dahlia into the center front of the 8-in/20-cm tier. Create two bundles of peonies, filler flowers, leaves, and berries. Twist the wires together, and then wrap with floral wire. I insert these arrangements into plastic straws first and then insert into the cake with needle-nose pliers. This keeps the wires completely separate from the cake. Always remember that it is dangerous for wires to come in contact with cake. The moisture from the cake can cause a reaction, and chemicals can be released into the food product. Insert these arrangements to the left of the large dahlia, at about 7 o'clock, so that the arrangement appears to be at a slight angle, and to the right side of the large dahlia at about 2 o'clock. Add more berries, filler flowers, and leaves to fill in any holes as shown.

Place a large peony on the top tier of the cake. Surround the peony with small arrangements of blackberries, filler berries, filler flowers, and leaves, covering the entire top tier.

Baker's Secret

If you wish to display a cake on a platter instead of a board, as I did for this cake, you will need to stack the cake upon delivery. Insert an offset spatula under the bottom tier; lift it up so you can get your hand under the cake and place onto the platter. Repeat process with the other tiers, stacked on top of each other. Then attach your flowers as directed.

GOLDEN BIRTHDAY CAKE

This cake is great for a golden birthday, anniversary, or even a wedding. You can take these elements and pare them down for smaller cakes if needed.

Supplies:

6-in/15-cm cardboard round

14-in/35-cm finished cake board

4 lbs/1.8 kg ivory fondant

Gold luster dust (I recommend Albert Uster brand)

Gold pearl dust

Gold dragées

Fat straws or dowels

Pearl border mold

Multistrand pearl mold

Large jeweled brooch mold (2 in/5 cm or larger)

Small brooch mold (1 in/2.5 cm)

Fondant with tylose: ivory, white, and gold ivory
   (about 1 lb/454 g each)

1½-in /3.8-cm square cutter

Straightedge

X-ACTO knife

Scroll mold

Golden ivory gumpaste

Lollipop stick

Foam square

Gum glue Isomalt

Number stamps

Toothpick

Hand torch

Cakes, (torted, filled, frosted):
   One 12 in/30 cm
   Two 8 in/20 cm
   One 6 in/15 cm

Begin with your two 8-in/20-cm round tiers of cake. Insert a fat straw into the center of one of the tiers. Mark with your finger or pen and pull out. Trim the straw. Cut five more straws to the same length, being careful that the cuts are straight across and all equal height. Insert all the straws into the base cake tier.

Apply a thin, even layer of buttercream on top of the straws, and place the second 8-in/20-cm round on top of the base. This configuration is called a double-barrel tier. Apply a thin coat of buttercream over the entire surface of the cake.

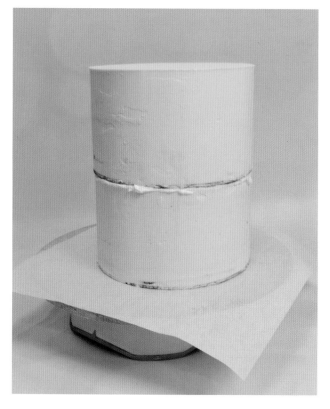

Use your tall bench scraper to remove the excess buttercream. Smooth out the top edge with an offset spatula. Place the cake back into the refrigerator until the buttercream is fully chilled before covering in fondant.

To cover in fondant, you can use one of two methods. You can use the Traditional Technique (see page 58), or you can use the Paneling Method (see page 67). You will need a full batch of fondant rolled out to a thickness of ¼ in/.63 cm. If you are using the Traditional Method, make sure you smooth out the top immediately after you place the fondant on the cake, and press in the edges to prevent it from cracking under the weight of the loose fondant pulling down on the sides.

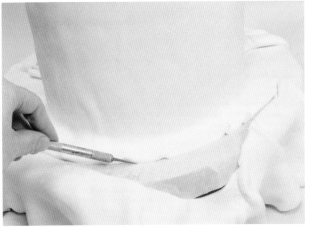

Baker's Secret

You may notice the center cardboard round showing through the fondant. For this design, that is not an issue because it will be covered by the bow. For other cake designs, if you wish to hide this line, trim the bottom board of the top 8-in/20-cm round down ¼ in/.63 cm, so when you fill with the buttercream, the cardboard will be hidden.

Cover your 6-in/15-cm round with fondant using the Traditional (see page 58) or Upside-down Technique (see page 64), depending on your preference. Chill cake before stacking.

The 12-in/30-cm bottom tier of the cake will be paneled so that the top can be a different color from the sides. Follow the instructions for paneling on page 67. Panel the top of the cake white and the sides in a golden ivory color. Next, brush gold luster dust onto the sides of the tier. For easy cleanup, place a piece of plastic wrap under your cake to catch any dust while you are brushing. Use a medium-sized fluffy brush, load it with your dust, and tap off the excess into the container. Apply in small circles with even pressure. There will be some variation in coverage. After dusting, use a small offset spatula to gently pick up the cake and place on top of your prepared board. Carefully center your cake on the board and set down. I chose ivory for my board, with a white ribbon.

Roll out some white fondant to about ⅕ in/5 mm. Use the square cutter to cut some squares. Let these set so that they are easy to handle and do not stretch when you pick them up. Cut a few in half to use for the first row. Attach squares with a little water. Leave a space between each square (about ⅛ in/3 mm). Continue placing squares upwards, leaving equal space between the squares.

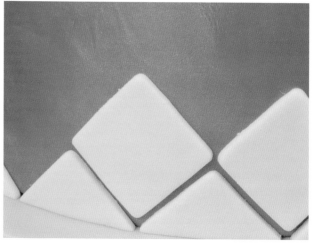

To keep tiles aligned, use a straightedge to place a few at a time as shown. Once the entire tier is covered, use your modeling tool to put lines in the corners of each square to create the appearance of tufting. With a bit of water, attach gold dragées to the cake where the points meet. Press the dragées into the surface of the fondant to secure.

Use your golden ivory fondant and the pearl border mold to create some pearl strands. The easiest way to do this is to roll out a small-sized snake and press into one end of the mold, and then continue on until you have the entire mold filled. Pinch off the excess. Pop the fondant out of the mold and apply to top and bottom edges of the cake with a little water. (To avoid having your fondant stick in the mold, dust the mold with a bit of cornstarch first before inserting your fondant.) Chill cake before stacking.

After your bottom tier is chilled, insert your fat straws as you did with the double barrel. Use an 8-in/20-cm round pan to find the center of the tier, and then lightly trace a line around the pan with a modeling tool so you know where to place the straws. This time use eight straws to support the weight of the double barrel. Place the double barrel on top of the bottom tier. Because it is chilled, you should be able to lift it gently with your hands placed flat on the sides of the cake. Centering it over your traced circle on the bottom tier, place the double barrel on top.

Trace a 6-in/15-cm pan on the top of your double barrel, same as above, and then insert five fat straws as shown into the top of your double barrel to support your final tier.

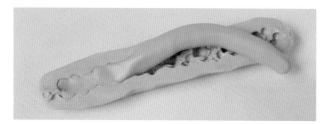

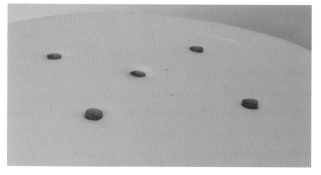

Roll out a thin piece of ivory fondant that is about 10 in/25 cm in length and 8 in/20 cm wide. Coat the front of the cake in a thin layer of shortening so the ivory fondant will stick to it but be able to be adjusted easily without tearing too much.

Roll the fondant onto a pipe or rolling pin, and lay it against the front of your cake. Starting from the bottom and working your way up, press the fondant into the ledges so it lies flat. Use a ruler to find the center of your piece of fondant, and mark the top and bottom. Starting at the top point, cut a gently curving line from the point to the top of the second tier using an X-ACTO knife. Do not cut too deep, or you will go through both layers of fondant. Create another curve from the top of the second tier to the bottom point. Repeat the curve on the opposite side of the fondant. If you need a template, see page 218. Pull off the excess fondant.

Place some plastic wrap around the base of your second tier to protect it from falling gold dust. Dust the front panel of ivory with your super gold pearl dust. Mark a dot down the side of the gold panel on the top tier every 2 in/5 cm or so. Make sure they are equal height. Use a straightedge to connect the dots in a laced pattern. These marks will be your guide for placing the laces.

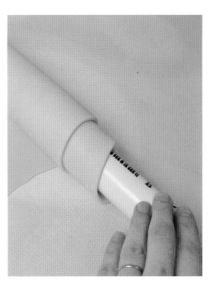

Roll out some more of the white fondant to ½₁₂ in/3 mm thick. Use a straightedge to cut laces that are about ¼ in/6.5 mm wide. Starting at the top, place the first lace straight across. The successive laces will follow the pattern you mapped out with your straightedge. Cut off the excess fondant as you go. The bottom lace should also be straight across.

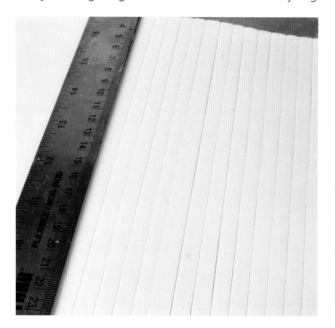
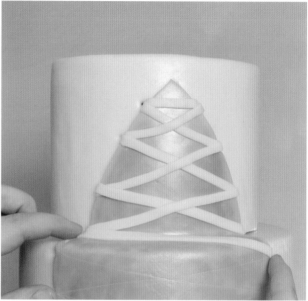

Roll out a thin piece of the golden ivory fondant. Use a straightedge and cut four pieces of fondant that are roughly 2 in/5 cm wide and 8 in/20 cm long. On two of the pieces, roll the top edge over. Place one end at the edge of the golden panel and wrap around the side to the back center of the cake tier. On the second piece of fondant, roll the top and the bottom edge and place over the bottom edge of the first piece of fondant.

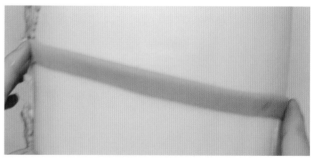
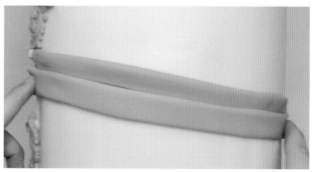

Roll out another thin piece of fondant. Cut the fondant into a rectangle and then split into four pieces.

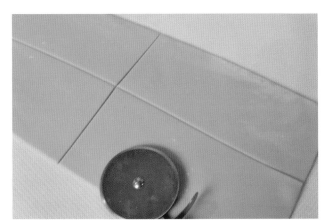

Cut a V out of the bottom edge of one piece. These will be the ribbons of the bow.

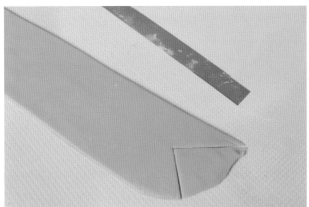

Attach to the back of the cake where the two ribbons that wrapped around the sides meet.

Gather the edges of another rectangle of fondant, fold over, and pinch together to make one half of the bow. Attach to the back of the cake.

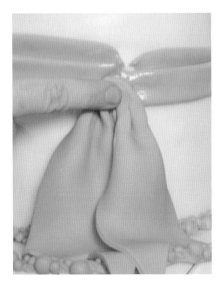

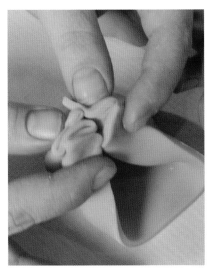

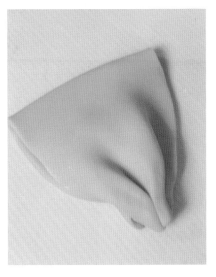

Repeat with two other rectangles and attach as shown.

Place some golden ivory fondant into your scroll mold in the same fashion as the pearl mold. Push into the mold starting at one end, and work your way to the end, pinching off the excess. Use a small rolling pin to press the fondant flat and firmly into the mold. Gently bend the mold to reveal the molded fondant, and place around the edge of the golden panel. Finish adding the pearl border around the base and top edge of the tiers.

Finish the cake by combining some gold dust and some vodka or lemon extract. Make sure you don't add too much liquid. The mixture should be thick. Paint the bow and trim with a small paintbrush. While painting, tilt the bowl to the side and use the gold dust that has settled on the bottom of the bowl. It will coat the fondant better than the liquid on top because it is more concentrated. Note: Not all gold dusts are created equal. Some are labeled "edible" and some are not. I prefer using the Albert Uster gold dust. It is non-toxic but not technically a "food," so therefore, I advise my clients to not eat the fondant that is gold. Besides, it gets all over your teeth and mouth if you eat it.

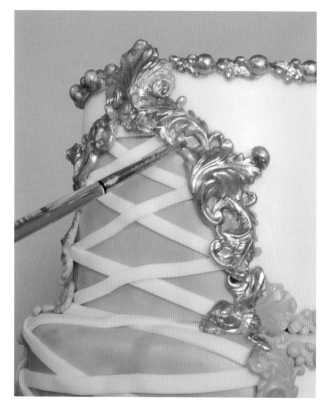 

Making the Crown

Roll out a round piece of white fondant that is about 2 in/5 cm tall. Flatten one side to be the base. Use your modeling tool to make six indentations. Place onto a lollipop stick inserted into a foam square. Attach a small piece of golden ivory gumpaste on top of the white ball. Cut off the excess stick. Roll out a thin piece of golden ivory gumpaste, trim into a square that is twice as tall as your white ball of fondant, and cut out some skinny triangles as shown.

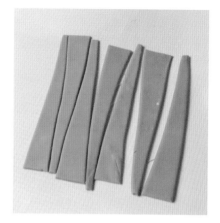

Roll up the skinny tips of each triangle. Apply some gum glue to the base of the white ball. Attach the wider end of the triangle to the base as pictured, and then attach the rolled tips to the top with some gum glue. Use small pieces of plastic wrap to hold up the pieces of gumpaste, and let them dry overnight or until firm. Once the crown is firm, remove the plastic wrap. Paint the crown with the gold dust paint.

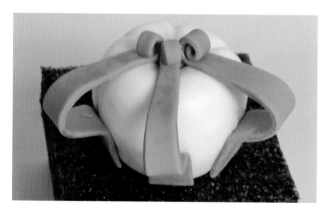

Roll out a small piece of gumpaste, and cut out a small circle. Using stamps, indent the circles with numbers appropriate for the birthday or anniversary being celebrated. Let dry for a few hours until firm. To assemble, apply some gum glue to the back of the circle; lay a toothpick over the back as pictured. Roll out some gumpaste into a skinny snake, and attach around the edge of the circle. Cut off the excess. Apply more gum glue and attach the other circle to the back.

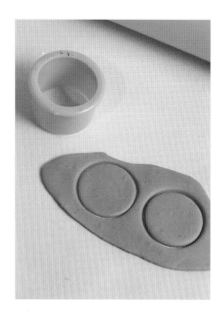
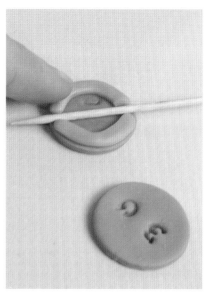

Push some white fondant into your pearl mold, remove the pearls from the mold, and attach to each part of the crown with some gum glue. After you have attached all the pearls, paint the nonpearl parts with gold to match the crown.

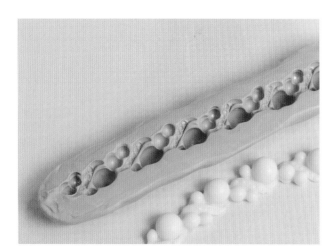

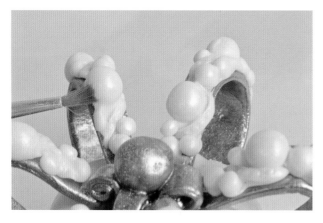

Place the number topper on top of the crown. Finish off with another white piece of fondant rolled into an oblong pearl for the top.

Make a small brooch by inserting a small piece of white fondant into the area where the gem is in the small brooch mold. Insert some golden ivory fondant on top and press flat. Remove carefully and attach to the crown in between the pearl arches. Attach some pearls around the outside edge. Mold some golden ivory fondant using your multistrand pearl mold, and wrap it around the base of your crown. Paint any remaining crown areas of golden ivory in gold. Place your finished crown on top of your cake.

To make a small brooch for the back of the bow, melt some ready-made pearl isomalt in a silicone cup for 15-second increments until melted. If bubbling, wait for the bubbles to settle down. Then pour into the mold, filling only the gem area with the pearl isomalt. I am using a brooch mold here from Marvelous Molds that is safe for hot sugar. Melt some gold isomalt in the same way and pour over the top. Once cooled (about 15 minutes), you can pop it out of the mold. Lightly torch to remove any surface bubbles. To attach to cake, see Pro Tip on page 169.

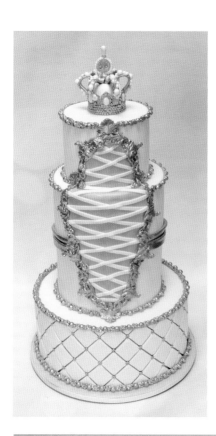

Pro Tip

Michelle Boyd

www.goodgraciouscakes.com

To attach an isomalt piece, like the brooch, to a cake, remelt some more of your gold isomalt and let thicken slightly. Dip a toothpick into the gold and attach to the back of your brooch. Make sure you wear gloves so the oil from your hands does not leave fingerprints. You can now insert the brooch into the cake.

CHAPTER 8
SCIENCE OF STRUCTURE

Structured cakes are ones that are actually the shape of the 3-D item you are trying to re-create. They are typically not stacked and need some sort of internal support structure (like a skeleton) to hold the cake in place. Sometimes this internal support can be fairly simple, and other times, it is quite complex. No matter what cake design you wish to create, there is an internal structure that will make it possible. The key is understanding how to construct the structure and what edible materials are best going to support it. The most efficient way to do this is to sketch out a skeleton of your cake's structure, and take it with you to the hardware store. Compare what's in your structure drawing to the various pipes, fittings, and wires available. You might even want to ask someone at the store for assistance, telling them what you want to make—just be prepared for some strange looks when you tell them it's for a cake! There are a lot of potential materials out there that could be used for structure. The more you familiarize yourself with them, the more ideas you'll have about what you can make and how to do it.

After I sketch out my cake design, I decide what parts will be cake, what will be Rice Cereal Treats (RCT) or aluminum foil, and what parts will be modeling chocolate or other edible materials. This helps me understand my cake design even better. The more you understand your design, and the more refined your plan is before you start, the better your chances of succeeding. Another factor to keep in mind is how many servings of cake you need in proportion to the design.

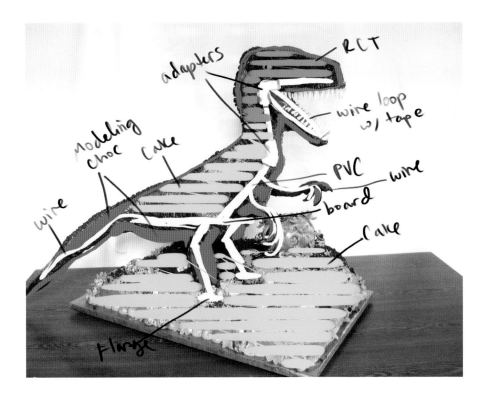

EDIBLE ELEMENTS

It's also important that the edible products you choose work for a structured cake. Whipped cream and champagne cake, for example, are very delicate and not a good idea for a structured cake. Modeling chocolate can be very strong unless it's very hot outside; then you can have problems with melting. Fondant stays flexible, but is heavy. If your structure is not strong enough to support a 100 percent fondant covering, you can get sagging. Rice cereal is a great way to bulk up an area that does not have to be cake and is completely edible, but it can be tricky to mold and needs time to set before you can add on decorative elements. Always consider your environment and your schedule when building your structure.

The following photos are some examples of sculpted cakes. The yellow area represents cake. The blue area is rice cereal treats (RCT) or aluminum foil filler. The pink area is modeling chocolate or fondant. You can see where all the structures are and how the cake will be supported. Do not leave these details to figure out after you already have started the cake. Sometimes I do a "mock" stacking of the cake by putting together the structure and then, with the structure in front of me, visualizing where the cake and the other edible elements will be.

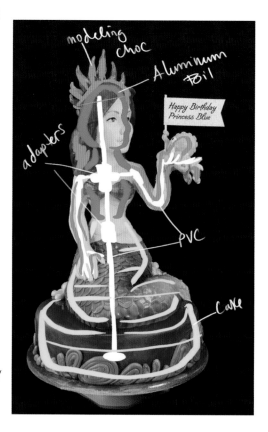

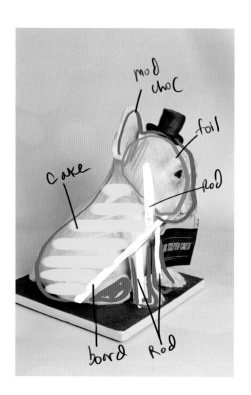

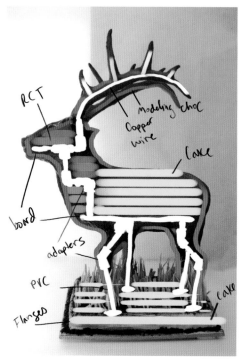

These are some of the common edible elements I use most often in my cake structures:

Rice cereal

Marshmallows

Royal icing

Chocolate

Modeling chocolate

Ganache

Buttercream

Fondant

Gumpaste

STRUCTURE SUPPLIES

Below you will find a photo and a description of the tools and supplies I use most often to make structured cakes. Don't let this list limit you. You might find something that works even better for the cake you want to create. Just make sure that the items you use are food safe and that you clean and cover them properly before using for a cake.

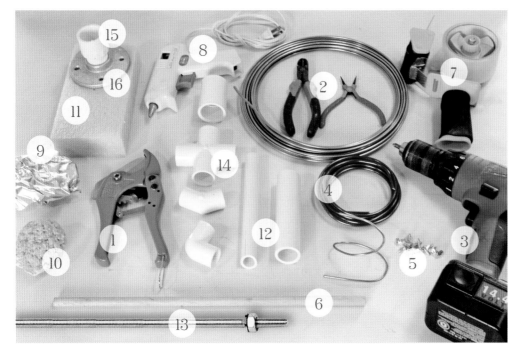

Note: *Most of these supplies can be found in the plumbing section of your hardware store.*

Tools

1. PVC cutters
2. Wire cutters
3. Drill

Common Supplies

4. Wire (copper, aluminum, various gauges—the higher the number, the thinner the wire).
5. ¼-in wood screws
6. Wooden dowels
7. Clear packing tape
8. Hot glue
9. Aluminum foil
10. Rice cereal treats (RCT)
11. Foam

PVC

12. Pipes (come in different widths, can be cut to any length). Clean with soapy water and cover with tape before use.

Threaded Rod

13. Threaded rod is very thin and very strong and should be cut to size at the hardware store. Secure with washers and nuts.

Adapters

14. These come in various sizes and configurations that enable cut pieces of PVC to be attached together to create differently shaped structures.

15. Male adapter—screws into the flange so that PVC pipe can be inserted.

Flanges

16. Made of metal. Screw into the base board to anchor the structure to the board. Male adapters are screwed into flanges first so the structure can be built up from the flange. These come in various sizes.

PLANNING AHEAD

The following is an abbreviated example of the process of making a cake that has a sculpted part. That part is made in advance and then combined with the cake portion. This is a very common practice in structured cakes. Since some elements of a cake may take quite a while to detail, do those parts first. The goal is for the cake portion to be as fresh as possible. In this cake, the head portion may take up to a week to create and fully detail, so you want to do that first, and then add it to your cake when it is finished.

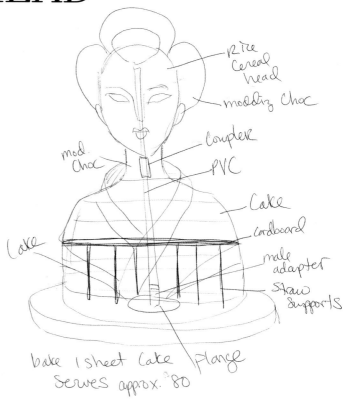

Labels on drawing: Rice Cereal head · moddlng Choc · Coupler · PVC · Cake · cardboard · male adapter · Straw Supports · mod. Choc · Cake · bake 1 sheet Cake Flange Serves approx. 80

MAKING RICE CEREAL TREATS

For this cake bust, the head is made of rice cereal treats (RCT). This is a wonderful medium for structured cakes because it is lightweight, carvable, and completely edible.

There are a couple of tricks for making RCT. I don't use a recipe, first of all. I usually take half of the mini marshmallows from a bag and melt them in a large microwave-safe bowl (allow for expansion during heating), until they are very, very melted—in the same fashion as if I were making fondant. Use a spatula to smear the melted marshmallows onto the area where you want the rice cereal to stick. Let it cool. This edible glue will keep your rice cereal attached to your structure.

To make the RCT, take the remaining marshmallows and melt them in the microwave, heating on high for 30-second intervals and stirring in between, until they are very melted and hot. Mix in approximately 4–6 cups/85–128 g of rice cereal. You want the consistency to be sticky but not too gooey. Make sure all the cereal is evenly coated. Add more cereal as needed until you have a pretty stiff consistency. Let cool for 5 minutes or until you can pick up a clump and it sticks together by itself. If you try to work with the cereal right away, it will not hold its shape.

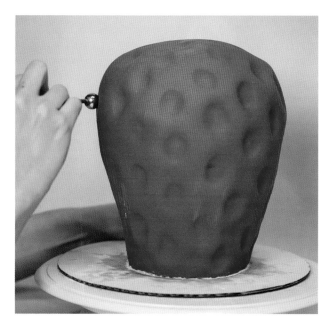

With a ball tool, make some divots into the surface of your cake. Airbrush the divots with red airbrush coloring mixed with some brown to develop depth, or use some dark red petal dust in the divots. Paint a little white food coloring onto the top of the cake with a brush at the spot where the stem attaches to the berry. The red will bleed through a bit and make it appear a little pink. This is okay.

Combine a little yellow and brown fondant together and shape into small teardrops. These will be the seeds on your strawberry. Use a little gum glue to attach the seeds to the cake. Place the cake onto the cake board (see page 144). Finish with a light spray of vodka to bring out the shine.

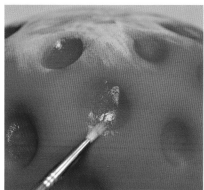
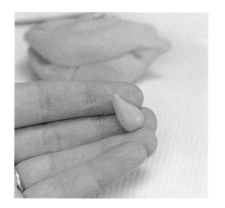

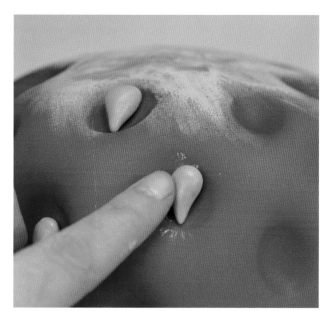

Now it is time to add the details—this is my favorite part. First, create a border around the base of the cake to hide the seam. Roll out a piece of green fondant, and cut out a grassy border. Use your X-ACTO knife to cut some random pointy shapes. Place this border around the base, and attach with a little water.

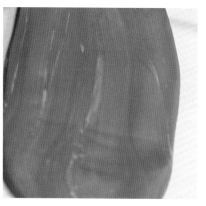 

Knead some brown and leftover yellow fondant together, but do not blend it all the way. This is what we will use to make a brown door to the strawberry house. Roll it out to about a ¼-in/6-mm thickness, and trim into a rectangle. Use your modeling tool to add some lines to the door to make it look like it's paneled. Cut a few skinny pieces of fondant and attach to the door to look like cross beams. Attach to the strawberry house with a little gum glue or water. Cut out some white fondant circles and attach to the cake with some water. These will be the windows.

 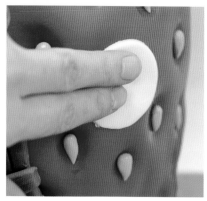

Roll out some brown fondant into a thin snakes. Twist together and make the tip pointy. These will become branches around your windows. Apply a little gum glue to the window around the edge, and make a cross in the center of the window. Form a few small green leaves by shaping small teardrops, flattening them, and using your modeling tool to mark a line down the center. Attach your branches of twisted fondant around the window as pictured, and then attach your leaves. This will make your windows appear to be made from tiny branches and leaves.

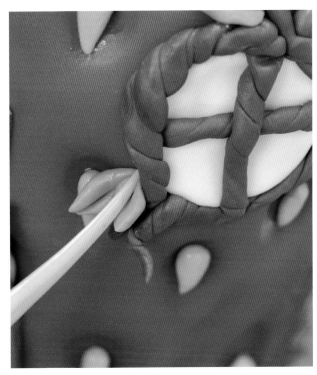

Now attach the leafy top you made earlier. Add some green petal dust to your leaves to give them some depth. Apply a little gum glue to the top of the cake to make it sticky. Press on a circle of green fondant. Then attach the leaves to the circle by wetting the fondant slightly with a little gum glue and pressing each leaf into it. Roll out some more green fondant into a fat snake. Cut off the ends. Pinch the tips of one end as shown to make the stem of the strawberry.

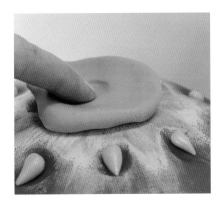

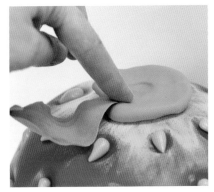

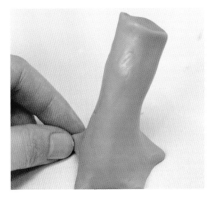

Glue the stem on top of the leaves with a little more gum glue. Insert a lollipop stick into the base of your stem if it is not staying upright, or add a little more tylose powder to the fondant to stiffen it up. Texture your stem with your modeling tool. Combine some ivory and brown fondant to marble it, but do not combine fully. Roll out some various-sized balls and press flat with your fingers. Attach to the board in front of the door to create some stepping stones. Put the mushroom stems and caps together with a little gum glue, and then attach to the cake board with more gum glue.

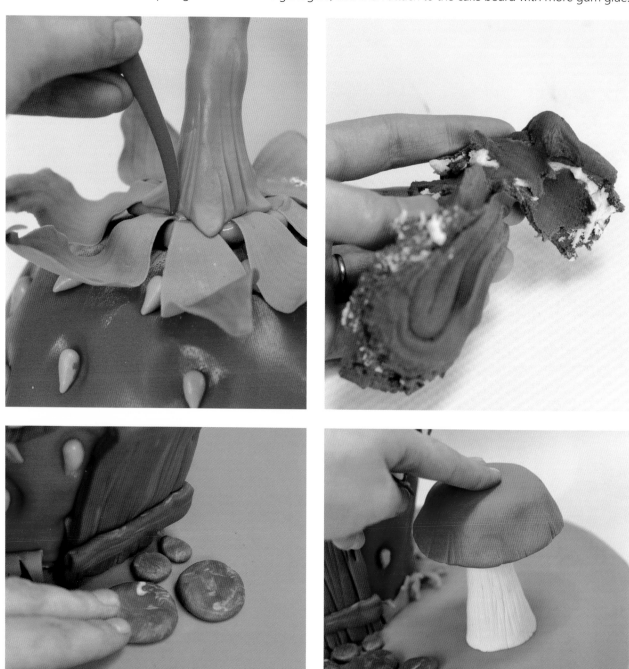

I added a few dots of white to make the mushrooms spotted. You could also paint on the dots with some white food coloring. Place one of your hydrangea flowers on top of the strawberry next to the stem and then a couple of others near the door. Once the dots on the mushroom are dry (in about an hour), you can carefully place your fairy from Chapter 5 onto the mushroom with a little gum glue. Your strawberry fairy house is now complete.

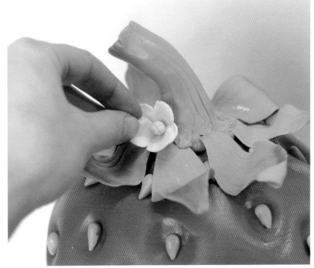

PRO PROJECT: HOT-AIR BALLOON CAKE

This is a fun sculpted cake that will take your sculpting skills to the next level. This structure is also the one I use the most. A lot of structured cakes can be made with one center support pipe and then various supporting boards in between the cake layers. The sketch here maps out where all the supports will be and also shows the plan for all the elements needed for this cake.

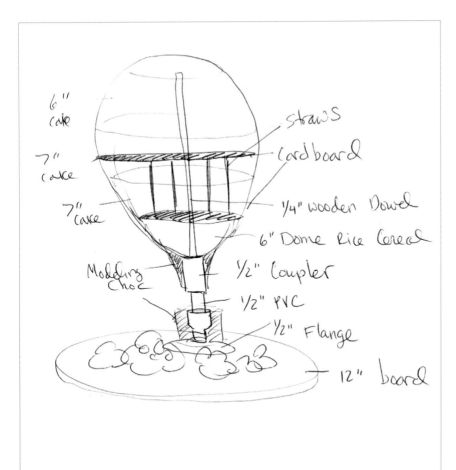

Structure:

12 in/30 cm board

½-in/1.25-cm flange

½-in/1.25-cm male adapter

½-in/1.25-cm PVC pipe

½-in/1.25-cm coupler

¼-in/.63-cm wooden dowel

1 toothpick

Fat straws

6-in/15-cm cardboard round

8-in/20-cm cardboard round
    (trimmed to 7 in/17.5 cm)

Packing tape

6-in/15-cm ball pan

Edible Supplies:

Cakes (chilled):
    Two 7 in/17.5 cm
    One 6 in/15 cm

1 batch SMBC Buttercream
    (see recipe, page 34)

Approximately 8 oz/227 g
    modeling chocolate

Fondant, with tylose added: light
    blue and dark blue, red, white,
    ivory, and brown

Rice cereal

Marshmallows

Special Tools:

2-in/5-cm circle cutter

Basket weave impression mat

Round scalloped cutter

Toothpick

Begin by assembling your structure as pictured below. Prep your board with poster board feet. Place the flange in the center of the board, and screw into place. Screw in the male adapter. Cut a piece of PVC pipe about 4 in/10 cm long. Attach a coupler on top of the PVC. You may glue these pieces together at this point, but it is not necessary for this structure. Cut the wooden dowel down to about 18 in/45 cm long. Insert it into the PVC pipe. Fill the area around the wooden dowel (inside the PVC pipe) with hot glue to secure. Grease your ball pan (a bowl of the same size would also work) and lay a piece of plastic wrap inside the bowl. Make a RCT mixture (see page 174) of about 2 cups/99 g marshmallows, melted and combined with enough rice cereal to form a stiff mixture. Let cool a few minutes until it sticks together when you pick it up. Press into the pan and compact. Use a cardboard round to flatten the top. Insert a piece of the dowel down the center to create a hole. Remove the dowel. Let cool overnight.

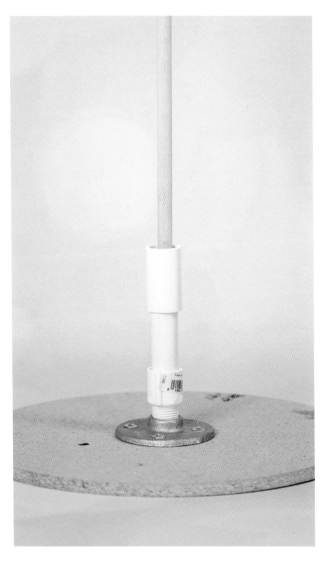

Once the RCT is cooled, you can remove from the pan and place onto the structure. The PVC coupler should keep the RCT from slipping down further. If it's not, you can cut a small piece of cardboard the same width as the coupler and poke a hole into it. Insert it over the dowel and onto the coupler, and then place the RCT on top of the cardboard.

Cut an X with an X-ACTO knife into the center of your 6-in/15-cm cardboard round. Place on top of the RCT. Place all your layers of cake onto the cardboard round for now. This is just a prestack. Do not place buttercream between the layers yet. Use a lid or a cardboard round to help guide your carving. You are trying to achieve a round shape. Since cake tends to compress after you put buttercream and fondant on top, you should carve a slightly oval shape, so that when it compresses, the cake will be fairly round. Place your cake onto a turntable for easy carving. Put a piece of plastic wrap over your base to catch carved cake. Begin carving your cake off in small pieces, working your way around. Check the cake's shape against your round model often to see where you need to take off more cake.

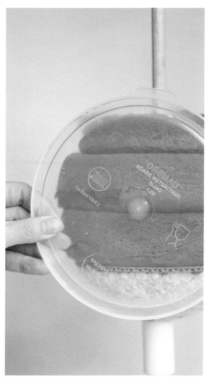

Once your cake is carved, mark where the top of the cake is against the dowel. Remove your sculpted cake by lifting the cardboard round off the dowel. Trim off the excess dowel with wire cutters.

Tort your cakes and restack onto your structure. This time, spread buttercream between your layers as you stack (you could also use ganache if you prefer). When you get to the middle of the cake stack, insert four equal-length straws into the cake so they are level with the top of the cake, and then insert the trimmed 7-in/17.5-cm cardboard round by cutting an X into the center of the cardboard and placing on top of the cake. Glue board down with a little buttercream. Continue stacking and filling the rest of the cake in this fashion. Crumb coat the cake with a thin layer of buttercream.

Take a small amount of modeling chocolate, and wrap it around the base of the RCT layer. This is to create the bottom part of the hot air balloon. Smooth the top part of the modeling chocolate into the RCT and the PVC so that it appears to be a seamless transition from the RCT to the pipe (as shown). Use some shortening on your fingers or a bit of water to smooth the modeling chocolate. Place the cake into the refrigerator overnight, or at least for a few hours until the buttercream is completely firm.

If you have not glued your pipe into the male adapter, you can carefully lift the pipe and cake out and place into your sculpted cake holder (Chapter 8, see page 176) so you can cover your board in fondant. If you chose to glue the pipe in, you can roll out your fondant, cut a seam on one side, and wrap around the pipe carefully. Overlap your cut edges as you do when paneling a cake, and cut through both layers of fondant with an X-ACTO knife. Remove the excess and blend the seam together with a little shortening.

To finish the board, trim off the excess fondant on the edges. Roll out a 2-in-/5-cm-wide piece of blue fondant about ⅛ in/3 mm thick and wrap it around the PVC pipe. Attach with a little water, and trim off the excess.

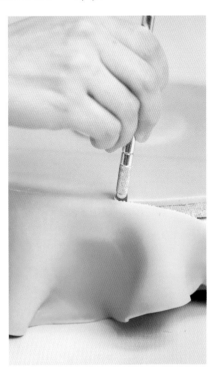

Roll out a piece of modeling chocolate that is about ¼ in/6 mm thick. Trim to 2 in/5 cm wide and about 6 in/15 cm long. Cut one end straight and wrap around the male adapter. This will be the basket. Trim off the excess and blend the seam.

Coat your balloon in a second layer of buttercream or ganache. Because this is a curved surface, and you want it to be perfectly smooth, put on a pair of gloves, and use your hands to smooth all the lumps and bumps out of the surface. Then chill the cake again for about 30 minutes. It will then be ready for you to cover with fondant.

Roll out about a half batch of LMF Fondant (see recipe, page 37) to ⅛ in/3 mm thick. Roll onto a rolling pin and carefully unroll onto your chilled cake. Begin smoothing the fondant at the top, and carefully work your way down. The fondant will start to get really thin the closer you get to the bottom of the cake, and you may get some tearing, but don't worry about it too much, because you will cover most of the bottom with decorations. Trim off the excess fondant with a knife or scissors. If it really tears, you can pull off the fondant, reheat it, knead, and try covering again.

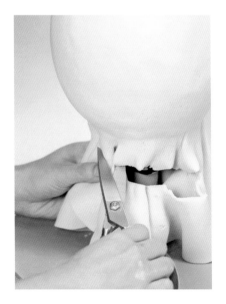

Roll out a piece of dark blue fondant and, using a ruler, cut a long ribbon about 1 in/2.5 cm wide and 6 in/15 cm long. Wrap around the base of the ballon

Use the template on page 218 to make some large shapes for the top and bottom of the balloon out of some thinly rolled red fondant. Apply them around the base of the balloon and the top with a bit of water. For the shapes for the base, trim off about 1 in/2.5 cm of the tip. Roll out a piece of light blue fondant and, using a ruler, cut a long ribbon about 1 in/2.5 cm wide and 18 in/45 cm long. Dust the top with a bit of cornstarch or powdered sugar to reduce sticking. Roll up into a spiral so you can easily unroll and attach it to the side of the balloon as shown. Make sure the seam is in the back, trim off the excess, and blend the seam.

Roll out some more red fondant (you can use your pasta machine to make this go faster) and use a small heart cutter to cut out about 12 hearts. Attach to the blue ribbon, evenly spaced, with a little water.

Roll out a snake of white fondant. Use the fondant smoother to roll it thinly to about the thickness of a shoelace. Begin attaching the rope around the edge of the red shapes at the bottom of the balloon, looping them over each other at the points as shown. Repeat the process at the top of the balloon.

Next, use the scalloped cutter to make a shape out of some thinly rolled white fondant. Attach to the top of the balloon with a bit of water.

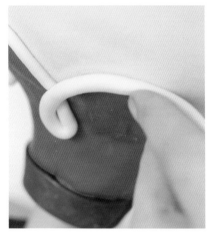

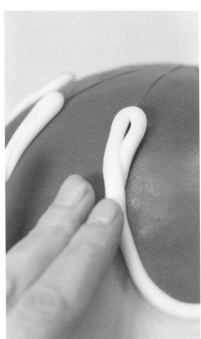

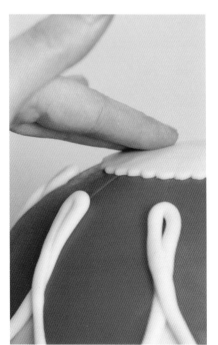

Roll out a thin piece of dark blue fondant and wrap it around the end of a tooth pick. Use a blade to trim the fondant into a triangle to make a small flag. Put a small ball of blue fondant at the base of the toothpick and insert into the top of the cake in the center of the scalloped piece.

Roll out some white fondant and place plastic wrap over it. Use the circle cutter to cut out some circles with the plastic wrap in place. (The plastic helps round out the edges of the fondant.) Fold the first circle in half and attach to the balloon just under the blue ribbon. Cut the second circle in half and attach on top of the folded circle as pictured. Use your modeling tool to create some tufted lines in the corners. Roll out some small balls of blue fondant and press between the points of the white tufts as pictured.

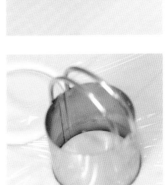

Roll out some brown fondant ⅛ in/3 mm thick, and press your basket weave texture mat into the fondant to imprint a texture. Use a ruler to measure, and cut a piece of the fondant 2 in/5 cm tall and about 8 in/20 cm long. Wrap the piece around the modeling chocolate basket created earlier, and attach with a bit of shortening or gum glue. Trim off the excess and blend the seam. Roll out a piece of brown fondant into a skinny snake in same manner used above for the white fondant. Fold in half and gently twist the two ends to create a spiral. Attach the spiral to the top of the basket with a bit of water. Trim off the excess. Roll out a small teardrop-shaped piece of white fondant. Attach to your basket with a bit of water. Create a couple of tufted lines with your modeling tool. Repeat with three more "bags," equally spaced around the basket.

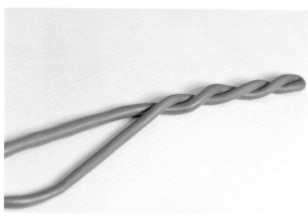

To make clouds, simply roll out varying sized balls of white fondant, and apply in bunches around the base of your basket and around the board. I usually make one big ball and surround it with a few smaller ones. Don't forget to stack some of the balls on top of each other to make puffy little clouds. Your cake is now finished. To serve, start from the top and cut down to the first carboard support. Cut slices as usual. Then remove the cardboard and go onto the next layer.

PRO PROJECT: OWL ON A BRANCH

. . . .

This cake may look intimidating, but it's easier to make than you might think. It's all about the structure in the branch and balancing weight. The owl appears to be out on a limb, balancing precariously, but it is actually perfectly placed right over the flange, so the weight is well supported. The head of the owl is made from RCT and the lower body from foam, both of which reduce the weight. Always think about how heavy cakes get when building structure. It's better to overbuild than to underbuild.

Structure:

14-in/35-cm heavy wooden base

½-in/1.25-cm flange

½-in/1.25-cm male adapter

½-in/1.25-cm PVC pipe

Two ½-in/1.25-cm elbow adapters, 135 degrees

One ½-in/1.25-cm elbow adapter, 90 degrees

T adapter with screw

Female adapter

6-in/15-cm foam egg

Copper wire

3 ft/9 dm anodized aluminum wire (available in craft stores in the floral department)

Packing tape

PVC glue

Two 6-in/15-cm cardboard rounds

Wooden skewer

Cake pop sticks

Edible Supplies:

Rice cereal

Marshmallows

50/50 (50% ivory fondant and 50% white modeling chocolate mixed together)

Dark modeling chocolate

Fondant, with tylose added: green, yellow, and black

Two 6 in/15 cm cakes (chilled)

Buttercream or ganache

Premade leaves from Chapter 6

Airbrush color or dusts

Special Tools:

Marvelous Molds Fur Texture Mat

1-in/2.5-cm round cutter

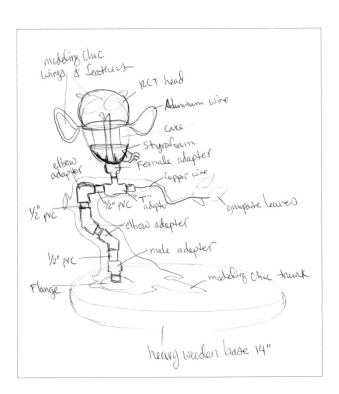

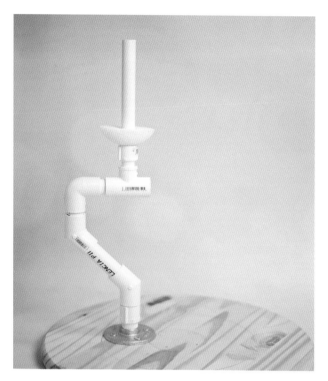

Start assembling the structure by gluing poster board squares to the bottom of your cakeboard. Attach your flange and your male adapter about 4 in/10 cm left of the center of the board. Cut four 2-in/5-cm PVC sections and one 3-in/7.5-cm section. Glue your PVC sections and adapters together, following the sketch on page 205. Attach an 8-in/20-cm PVC section to the top of the female adapter. Cover this section in packing tape to seal.

Cut the end off the foam egg with a carving knife. Use a piece of PVC pipe to make a hole in the foam end you removed. Place it onto a piece of cardboard and trace it (make two). Center a PVC pipe into the center, and trace around that as well so you know where to make an X. Cut the X and insert over the PVC pipe.

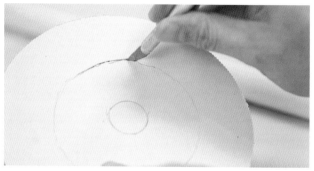

Tort cakes, fill with ganache, and trim away edges. Center your traced piece of cardboard in the center of the cakes, and glue down with a bit of ganache. Use it as a guide to carve a rounded top edge of the cake as shown. This will be the owl's body. Trim your PVC at an angle so it is pointed.

Place the cake onto the PVC pipe. Coat the layer in ganache, and let chill in the refrigerator overnight or until the ganache is set firm.

Make the RCT (see page 174). Mold some of the RCT into an oval. This will become the owl's head. Make sure it is wider than the owl's body. Place into a bowl to help keep its shape, and let set overnight.

Cover the PVC structure with packing tape to seal it. Melt the other half of the bag of marshmallows, and apply it to the surface of the pipe with a spatula. This is crucial because it gives the RCT something to stick to when you press it against the pipe. Prepare RCT the same way you did for the head. After it's cooled, press onto the surface of the pipe to create the tree trunk. Start at the bottom and work your way up.

Insert another 2-in/5-cm piece of PVC pipe into the T adapter. Take a 12-in/30-cm piece of copper wire and twist in half. Glue the bent end into the end of PVC pipe with hot glue. Cover with RCT as pictured. Make a small branch on the left side of the trunk. Attach with a bit of melted marshmallow if it does not stick to itself. Wrap the RCT with plastic wrap to hold it tightly against the PVC pipe and let set overnight.

Take a piece of your anodized aluminum wire, and thread it through the second marked cardboard round just below the center circle, as shown. Use the X-ACTO knife to cut an X in the circle, and place the cardboard onto the PVC and then skewer your RCT ball, which is the owl's head, onto the PVC. Trim the wire so that about 8 in/20 cm of wire sticks out on either side of the board. Bend the wire down towards the cake. Insert some cake pop sticks into the cake below the wire. Cover the wire in packing tape, and tape the sticks to the wire. Angle the wire slightly. These will be the wings of the owl. Cover the branch and trunk in modeling chocolate, and add textured lines with a modeling tool to mimic the look of bark.

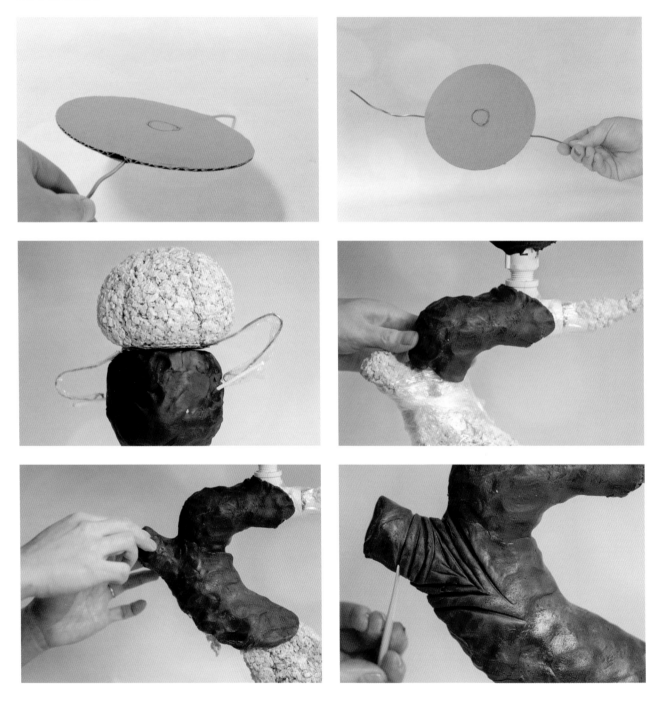

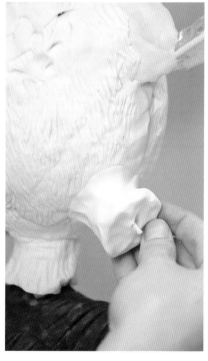

Begin covering the owl's body and head in the 50/50 mixture. Insert a skewer into the right side of the body to support the upraised foot. Cover the wings and the head as well. Use the Marvelous Molds Fur Texture Mat to add a feather texture to the surface. Cover the PVC under the cake with 50/50 to make the leg and texture with your modeling tool. Create a small cylinder and insert over the skewer as pictured for the extended leg. Blend the seam, and texture with a modeling tool.

Texture the legs with your mat as you did with the body.

Create a small half circle out of 50/50 and attach to the back for the tail. Smooth the seam with your modeling tool, and texture. Create the tufts of feathers over the eyes by forming a snake and then pointing the tip. Use a modeling tool to smooth the edges and blend into the owl's head. Use a modeling tool to create two detail lines as pictured. Start at the tip and pull the modeling tool towards the tip of the nose. This is to give the illusion of feathers.

Roll out a ball of 50/50 and flatten onto the front of the head into a slight teardrop shape as shown. Use the modeling tool to create texture lines that radiate from the center outwards. Use a ball tool to hollow out an area in the center for the eye.

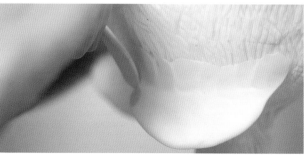

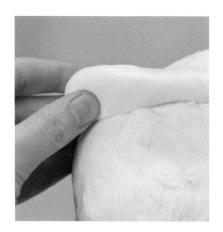

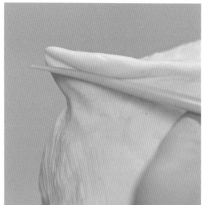

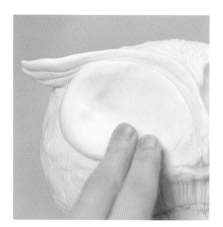

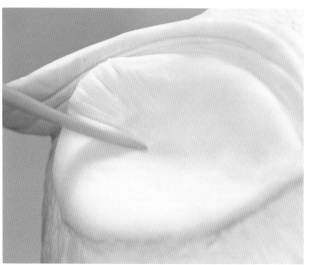

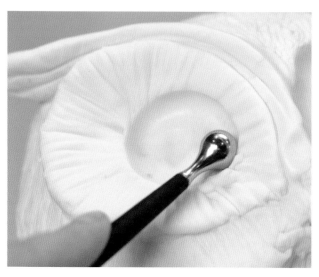

Roll out a ball of yellow fondant and insert it into the hollowed-out area of the eye. Use a small 1-in/2.5-cm round cutter to mark a spot on the eye that is towards the inside corner of the eye, not in the middle. Use a ball tool to slightly hollow out the marked area. Cut out a piece of black fondant with the same cutter, and insert into the hollowed-out area for the pupil, as shown. Roll out a black snake of fondant. Point the end. Attach to the outside edge of the eye with a bit of water. Wrap around the entire eye. Pinch off the excess and point the end. Attach at the corners. Hollow out one large spot and one small spot with your ball tool. Insert two pieces of ivory fondant cut with piping tips into the hollows to create highlights for the eye. You could also roll out small balls and just flatten into the hollows. Repeat these steps to make the owl's other eye.

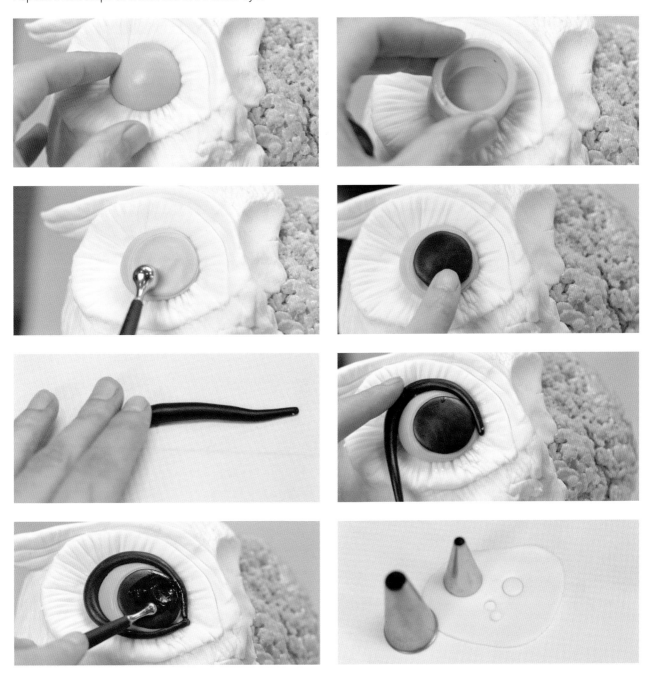

Add a fat snake of 50/50 to the bottom "cheek" area of the owl's head to add fullness and roundness to the head. Smooth the seam flat with a modeling tool and texture with the mat. Create a small hollow in the center between the eyes with a ball tool. Roll out a small teardrop shape from yellow fondant, and attach in the hollow to create the beak. Slightly build up the upper area of the wing with 50/50. Create some detail lines with your modeling tool as pictured. Roll out three small ropes of yellow fondant and attach under the leg to form the claws of the owl. Create three more and attach to the other leg with a bit of gum glue. Attach a fourth to the back of the three toes. Roll up a piece of plastic wrap and place under the foot against the branch to support the toes as they dry, or they will fall off.

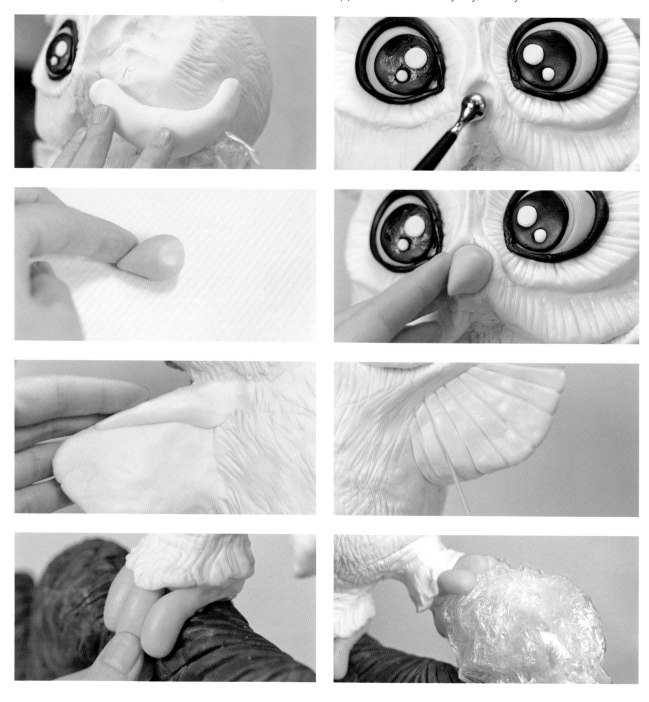

Coat your board in shortening. Roll out some green fondant and lay it on top of your board, working the edge around the roots of the trunk. Cut off the excess fondant at the edge. Continue laying on pieces of fondant. Overlap the edges and trim away with an X-ACTO knife, as you do when paneling. Blend the seam with your finger, and then texture the entire surface with your Marvelous Molds Mat to make it look like grass. Finish covering the stump with modeling chocolate. Create little hollows for roots, and continue adding texture lines with your modeling tool around the roots and over the surface of the trunk.

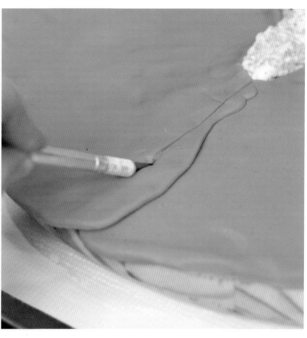

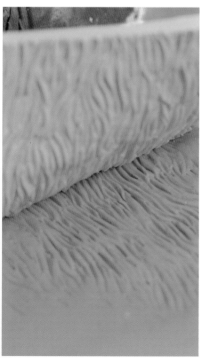

Finish your cake by adding some dimension to the owl's body and the grass. Apply a light coating of brown airbrush color around the edges of the body and to the creases of the owl's wings and head, to create dimension. Add dimension to the grass as well by airbrushing with the same color. Airbrush color darkens over time, so don't overdo it. Insert your premade leaves into the tips of the branches. Finish the cake with a light spray of water to seal in colors and get rid of any powdered sugar residue.

Baker's Secret

50/50 is a great medium to use for structure if you plan on airbrushing or adding color. If you try to airbrush modeling chocolate, the color will bead up. Fondant colors well, but it is very hard to blend the seams. 50/50 is able to take color, and the seams blend easily. It is the best of both worlds.

ABOUT THE AUTHOR

Elizabeth Marek has an AAS degree in Graphic Arts and worked in advertising before studying Pastry Arts at the Oregon Culinary Institute in Portland, Oregon. In 2007, she founded Artisan Cake Company.

Artisan Cake Company cakes have been featured in magazines such as *Portland Bride and Groom*, *CakeCentral Magazine*, and *Crave*. Her 3-D and sculpted cakes (often representing geek culture) have been featured on various website and blogs, such as Sunday Sweets, Squidoo, Boing Boing, Great White Snark, Cupcakes Take the Cake, and many others.

Elizabeth was included in *100 Steampunk Creations*, a book produced by Dr. Grymm and Barbe Saint John featuring steampunk art and creations. Elizabeth's steampunk cake won first prize in the CakeCentral competition, as did her gorgeous representation of the "hooded" figure T-shirt in the online Threadcakes competition.

Facebook: www.facebook.com/artisancakecoPDX
Twitter: www.twitter.com/artisancakes
Youtube: www.youtube.com/lizzomarek
Instagram: www.instagram.com/artisancakecompany
Tumblr: artisancakecompany.tumblr.com
Flickr: www.flickr.com/photos/artisancakecompany
Website: www.artisancakecompany.com

TEMPLATES

How to use these templates: Copy these templates on a scanner or copy machine and print out. You can enlarge or shrink as needed. Cut out or trace for your projects.

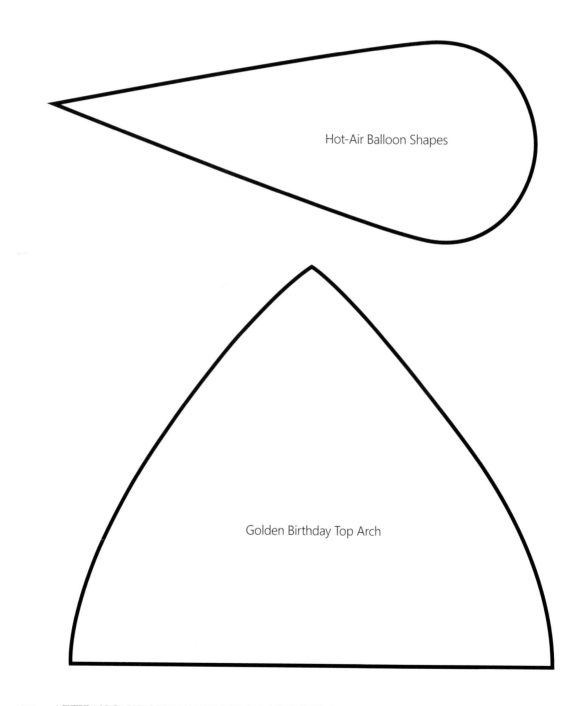

Hot-Air Balloon Shapes

Golden Birthday Top Arch

FAIRY TEMPLATE

Use these templates to calculate size and shape for the body, head, arms, and wings. Measurements for the support stick and foam block are also included.

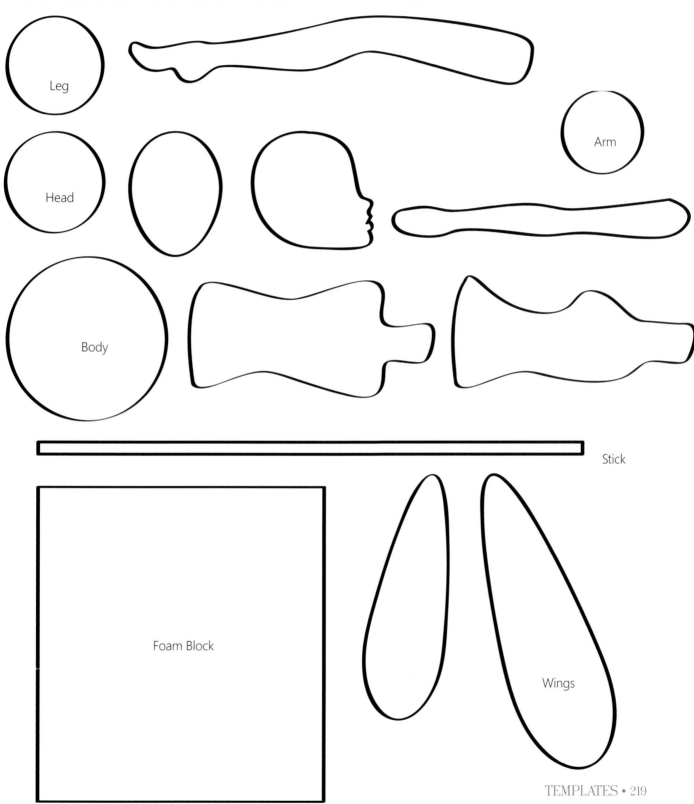

Leg

Arm

Head

Body

Stick

Foam Block

Wings

INDEX